The Forties and Fifties

An illustrated
History in colour
1945-1959

By
Nathaniel Harris

Special Adviser:
Dr J M Roberts
Fellow and Tutor in Modern History
at Merton College, Oxford

Macdonald Educational

The Forties and Fifties

Contents

4 In the Wake of War
6 Europe Divided
8 The Berlin Airlift
10 Rebuilding Europe
12 American Influence
14 The Welfare State in Britain
16 Indian Independence
18 Mao in China
20 The Birth of Israel
22 The Suez Crisis
24 War in Korea
26 From Stalin to Khrushchev
28 Sport and Adventure
30 Fad and Fashion
32 The Dawn of the Nuclear Age
34 Films of the Fifties
36 The United States: Pride and Prejudice
38 Peron in Argentina
40 Rock n' Roll
42 The Affluent Society
44 Cars
46 The Arts
48 Empires in Retreat
50 Science and Communication
52 Jets, Rockets and Space
54 The Main Events
56 Who Was Who
58 Project: Skiffle Band
60 Project: Understanding the Computer
62 Index
64 Further Reading and Acknowledgements

© 1975 Macdonald and Company (Publishers) Limited
49-50 Poland Street
London WLA 2LG

ISBN 0356 05089 0
Library of Congress Catalog Card Number 74-31819

Printed in Great Britain by: Morrison & Gibb Ltd London & Edinburgh

◄ **The war has ended** but great efforts will still have to be made, says this poster.

► **Elvis Presley,** King of Rock n' Roll, was a superstar of the fifties.

The forties and fifties were times of high hopes and terrible fears. The hopes were symbolised by the United Nations, set up at San Francisco in 1945. The fears centred on "the Bomb", a new weapon so frightful that the two dropped on Japan had been enough to end World War Two.

After this, although the United Nations did good work, war between the major powers never seemed far away. Two hostile blocs dominated the world: Communist Russia and her allies ("the East") and the United States and *her* allies ("the West"). But in spite of blockades, civil wars and a large-scale conflict in Korea, World War was avoided. By the end of the fifties "peaceful co-existence" seemed just possible.

The most dramatic change of the period was in living standards. In 1945 all the great powers except the U.S.A. were shattered; by 1959 an "age of affluence" was bringing undreamed-of prosperity to the masses in North America and Europe. But most peoples in Asia, Africa and South America had little share in the new wealth, though many became independent as the European colonial powers packed up and left.

The fifties saw great advances in science, with man himself about to move into space. Yet on earth many of his problems remained unsolved.

In the Wake of War

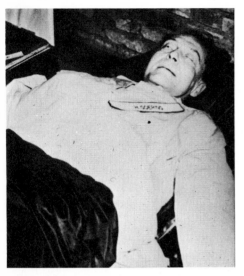

▲ **The body of Hermann Goering,** one of the top Nazi leaders. He was sentenced to death by the court at Nuremberg, but cheated the hangman by taking poison the night before his execution.

▼ **Wrecked trains at a German station,** good for nothing but scrap or firewood—which is probably what the two women are carrying off.

At the end of the Second World War in 1945, many countries were in ruins and the future seemed bleak.

Much of Europe had been heavily bombed from the air and fiercely fought over on the ground; cities had been reduced to rubble; atomic bombs had wiped out Hiroshima and Nagasaki in Japan. Millions were dead and many more were left homeless, jobless, and short of the essentials of life.

Europe was thronged with refugees and other "displaced persons". New governments and old hatreds stopped a number of them from going back to their homelands. Some, like many Poles in Britain, settled into a new life, but thousands lived in camps and found no country to take them in.

Among the displaced persons were many Nazi victims who had survived the concentration camps. The end of the war brought to light the full horror of Hitler's Germany, in which millions of innocent people had been murdered. At Nuremberg in Germany, Nazi leaders were put on trial for their crimes; most were found guilty and either hanged or sentenced to long terms of imprisonment.

The early post-war years were hard —and were made harder by the severe winter of 1946-7. There were still shortages of food and fuel, though rationing helped to keep people alive by sharing out what there was. Most countries suffered from lack of capital for rebuilding, from smashed communications, and from political troubles. And in spite of all their efforts, the signs and scars of war—ruined buildings, bitter feelings, drab clothing —lingered on for years.

Bicycle taxis appeared in Paris during the war, when there was almost no petrol available for private cars. They continued to be used for some time after the war; the supply of petrol continued to be short for a number of years.

▲ Political quarrels broke out soon after liberation. This Italian poster, ''Communism needs a boot'', can have two meanings: the ''boot'' can refer to Italy, which is roughly boot-shaped on a map, or to a good hard kicking that should be administered to Communism.

▼ Spivs were crooks who bought and sold ''black market'' goods (stolen or strictly rationed items). They did not include elephants, though the spiv here claims ''We can get 2/6 for them anywhere''.

▶ Queueing was part of the British way of life during and after the war—so much so that it was said an Englishman could join any queue he happened to see, out of pure habit.

Europe Divided

The wartime alliance between the Soviet Union and the West soon turned to rivalry. With Russia's victorious Red Army stationed over half of Europe, the continent was split in two.

▲ **Winston Churchill,** Britain's wartime Prime Minister, at Fulton, Missouri, where he told his audience "an iron curtain has descended across the continent". From then on the phrase "the iron curtain" was widely used.

In all the countries of Eastern Europe the Russians set up governments like their own, controlled by a Communist Party. This was done quite ruthlessly, even where most of the people were not Communist. Once established, these "People's Democracies" allowed no opposition to their governments, which in turn took orders from Russia.

This expansion of control, though justified by the Soviets in terms of national security, nevertheless alarmed the Western powers. And Communism seemed to be making steady progress. There were strong Communist Parties in Italy and France, and in Greece the Communists had been trying to carry out a revolution since 1944. At the same time, Communist hostility to the West was becoming obvious. An "Iron Curtain" sealed off Eastern Europe, and almost nobody was allowed in or out.

The U.S. President, Harry Truman, replied by putting forward the "Truman Doctrine". This stated that the U.S.A. in future would help any countries threatened by Communism outside the Iron Curtain. With American help the Greek Communists were crushed, but America could do little to stop a Communist takeover in Czechoslovakia in February 1948. There the Communists had been part of the elected government but, backed by the Red Army, still set up a dictatorship. To most people this proved that Communists were unbending enemies of democracy.

The growing tensions between East and West led to new military alliances; in March 1948 the Brussels Pact was signed between Britain, France and the Low Countries. The Berlin blockade (page 8) seemed to bring war very near, and the threat led the West to form a still wider alliance: N.A.T.O.

N.A.T.O.—the North Atlantic Treaty Organisation—involved the U.S. and Canada in the defence of Europe. At the same time, a new, non-Communist West German state was set up. Russia replied by setting up a Communist East German state.

The division of Europe was complete, and, in the years that followed, the two sides fought with propaganda and espionage. This was war of a sort, but not a "hot", shooting war; it is known as the "Cold War".

◄ **Men and women of E.L.A.S.,** the Communist-controlled Greek resistance army. They fought heroically against the Nazis and then took on non-Communist government troops in a savage civil war that lasted down to 1949; but for U.S. and British intervention they might have won.

NATO FORCES
25 Divisions in W. Europe
1000 Aircraft

COMMUNIST FORCES
25 Divisions in E. Europe
100+ Divisions in Russia
1000 Aircraft

Charter members of
NATO (+USA & Canada)

Communist bloc

'Iron curtain'

Centres of tension

| 0 Miles | 400 |
| 0 Kilometres | 700 |

Reykjavik ICELAND

NORWEGIAN SEA

NORWAY

SWEDEN

FINLAND

Helsinki

L. Ladoga

Oslo

Stockholm

BALTIC SEA

Moscow

DENMARK

GREAT

Copenhagen

RUSSIA

EIRE
Dublin

NORTH SEA

BRITAIN

NETH.

London   The Hague

Berlin

Warsaw

POLAND

ATLANTIC

OCEAN

Brussels
BELGIUM

WEST
GERMANY

EAST
GERMANY

Paris   LUX.

Bonn

Prague

FRANCE

GERMANY

CZECHOSLOVAKIA

Berne

SWITZ.

Vienna

Budapest

AUSTRIA

HUNGARY

RUMANIA

Trieste
(Free port)

Bucharest

BLACK SEA

Belgrade

PORTUGAL

Madrid

Corsica

YUGOSLAVIA

BULGARIA

Lisbon

SPAIN

Sofia

Rome

Tiranë

Ankara

Sardinia

ADRIATIC SEA

ALBANIA

GREECE

TURKEY

Tangier Gibraltar

Algiers

MEDITERRANEAN

Sicily

Athens

SPAN. MOROCCO

MOROCCO

ALGERIA

Tunis

SEA

Crete

CYPRUS

TUNISIA

Malta

▲ **Flashpoints of tension in Europe, 1948-9.**
Berlin. The most dangerous spot of all. The situation of West Berlin, a non-Communist city divided by war-time allies in the heart of Soviet occupation zone, was certain to cause trouble.

Vienna. Like Berlin, a partly Western city in Russian-occupied territory. But here agreement was easier, and in 1955 Austria became an independent and neutral country.
Belgrade. Yugoslavia was a Communist state but refused Russia unquestioning obedience.

In 1948 she broke with the Communist bloc, and for a time a Russian invasion seemed likely.
Trieste, with a mixed population, was fiercely disputed between Yugoslavia and Italy.
Paris and Rome. The strong French and Italian Communist Parties aroused fears of revolution.

7

The Berlin Airlift

Berlin was the scene of the first Cold War crisis, which revealed the West's determination to stand its ground.

The division of Germany into four occupied zones was only supposed to last until Nazism was rooted out and Germany formed into a peaceful democracy. But the growing suspicion between Russia and the West tended to split the country in two.

The American, British and French zones began to draw close together, and in 1948 a common currency was arranged for them. The Russians answered by blockading the Western sector of Berlin, the German capital. The city was deep inside the Russian zone, but because of its importance it had been divided between the four occupying powers.

Because of its position, the Russians could control all land traffic into and out of the city; and in June 1948 they refused to allow in any traffic from the West. Berlin was cut off, without essential supplies of food and fuel, and it looked as if the city would fall under Russian control unless the Western allies were prepared to fight.

Fortunately there was another way: Berlin could be supplied by air. The American and British air forces carried the enormous quantities needed into the city; by April 1949, some 1,400 flights were bringing in 8,000 tons of supplies every day. After eleven months, the blockade was lifted.

Berlin was saved, but Germany remained divided. The Western zones became West Germany (the Federal Republic), with Bonn as the new capital. East Germany became a Communist state, the German Democratic Republic, with East Berlin as its capital. West Berlin remained a danger spot, an isolated Western city behind the Iron Curtain.

▲ **The rugged and reliable Douglas C-47 Dakota.** The Dakota was the most widely-used military transport plane of World War Two, serving as freight transport, troop carrier and glider tug. During the airlift, American and British planes brought huge quantities of supplies into Berlin.

◄ **Millions fled to the West** in the last year of the war, either because they hated Communism or because they feared Russian revenge for wartime German atrocities. After the war the East German state set up by the Russians failed to win over the people, and thousands continued to cross to the West although they risked being killed by armed border guards. West Berlin, in the heart of East Germany, was the easiest place for refugees to reach, so that the city remained a centre of tension after the failure of the blockade.

▲ **The four sectors of Berlin,** surrounded on all sides by the Russian zone of Germany. The Russians could control entry to Berlin by road, rail and canal, and they probably believed it was impossible to keep a whole city alive by flying in supplies. But this was what the Western allies did, using the three airports marked on the map. The Russian blockade caused much suffering, but Berliners refused to register for food in the Soviet sector, or to hand over the administration of the city.

▲ **British troops loading coal** into a Dakota (see below) at Fassberg. The strain of round-the-clock flights was tremendous, but the airlift—"Operation Vittles"—was a success. Over two million tons of supplies, including food, fuel, clothing, machinery and even raw materials, were flown into Berlin, and goods produced in the city as exports were flown out to the West. About two-thirds of the flights were made by the American Air Force (U.S.A.A.F.) and one-third by the R.A.F.

Rebuilding Europe

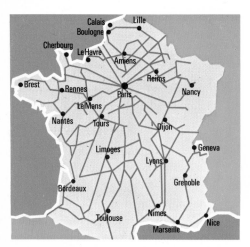

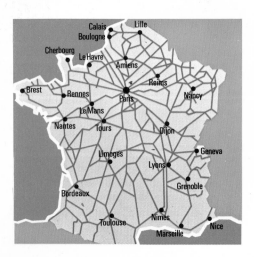

By 1948-9 life in Western Europe was returning to some sort of normality. Reconstruction was in full swing, the worst shortages were over, and democracy had been re-established.

Britain's Labour Government was putting through a programme of reforms. France was settling down under the Fourth Republic, though with rather weak governments. Italy had achieved stability. And West Germany had her first post-war elections in 1949. The Allied occupation ended in 1952, and within three years West Germany had re-armed and joined N.A.T.O.

European recovery owed much to the Marshall Plan, which operated from 1948 to 1952. But one of its effects was to harden European divisions, for Russia feared it was a plot to Americanise the Communist countries, and prevented them from accepting much-needed aid.

Marshall Aid was handled by the Organization for European Economic Co-operation (O.E.E.C.). A few years later, the European Coal and Steel Community was set up as a first step towards permanent economic co-operation. Finally, in 1957, the European Economic Community (E.E.C.) was formed, pledging its members to eventually abolish all trade barriers between one another.

The E.E.C., or Common Market, showed that ancient enemies—France and Germany—could work together. Other members were Italy, Belgium, Holland and Luxembourg; Britain, committed to the Commonwealth, would not join. But the Common Market signalled the end of post-war weakness and the birth of a new Europe.

▲ **The French rail network** was rapidly reconstructed. The maps show it in late 1944 (top), mid-1945 (middle) and May 1946 (bottom).

▲ **Goods reappeared in West German shops** from 1948, thanks to currency reforms and Marshall Aid. A healthy western Europe was impossible without Germany playing her part, though the German "economic miracle" of the fifties did revive some old jealousies and fears on both sides of the Iron Curtain.

▶ **"All colours to the mast".** This prizewinning poster was inspired by the European recovery carried out under the Marshall Plan. Its optimistic view of European co-operation was proved correct by the setting up of the Coal and Steel Community in 1951, which led on to the Common Market.

American Influence

▲ **President Truman** (centre) at the funeral of Franklin D. Roosevelt. Truman's tough, realistic policy involved sending U.S. troops, aid and advisers to many parts of the world.

The United States dominated the post-war period; no country had ever been so powerful and rich. The American way of life was envied and imitated throughout the non-Communist world.

In World War Two millions of ordinary Americans went abroad for the first time. The G.I. was well-supplied with everything from steaks and cigarettes to cars and silk stockings—luxuries no longer found in war-torn Europe, and completely new to most Asians.

Direct contact increased the influence of everything American, already familiar through Hollywood films and popular music. And Americans stayed on abroad after the war. U.S. bases appeared in many European and Asian countries, and the U.S.A. became the leading member of N.A.T.O. and other anti-Communist alliances.

American help also took the form of money, goods and technical assistance. In Japan even the political and educational systems were American-inspired. And from 1944 European reconstruction was carried out by the United Nations—two-thirds of the funds being supplied by the U.S.A.

When it became obvious that Europe needed far more help to recover, the Americans worked out a new scheme. The Marshall Plan, called after the American Secretary of State, involved pouring into Europe machinery and goods worth over thirteen million dollars. So strong was the American economy that it flourished in spite of all the money spent on aid, nuclear weapons and the forces abroad.

But there was another side to U.S. aid. The Americans' anti-Communism led them to help even governments which were corrupt or dictatorial, provided they were anti-Communist. They also interfered, secretly or openly, with other countries. (In 1954, for example, they trained and paid for an army to overthrow the reforming Guatemalan government.) Such actions led inevitably to anti-Americanism, especially in Latin America, Asia and the Arab world.

Christmas together... Have a Coca-Cola

...welcoming a fighting man home from the wars

Time of all times. Home at last...to wife, to child and to family. With Christmas in the air and the tree lighted brightly. All the dreams of a lifetime rolled into one moment. A home-like, truly American moment where the old familiar phrase *Have a Coke* adds the final refreshing touch. Coca-Cola belongs to just such a time of friendly, warm family feeling. That's why you find it in homes big and small across the nation...the drink that adds life and sparkle to living. A happy moment is an occasion for Coke—and the happy American custom, *the pause that refreshes.*

* * *

Our fighting men meet up with Coca-Cola many places overseas, where it's bottled on the spot. Coca-Cola has been a globe-trotter "since way back when".

-the global high-sign

"Coca-Cola" and its abbreviation "Coke" are the registered trademarks which distinguish the product of The Coca-Cola Company.

◄ **Coca-Cola and chewing gum** were symbols of the American way of life, as advertisers gleefully pointed out. American servicemen stationed abroad made them popular from Iceland to Japan.

► **"Free pass for the Marshall Plan"**, a German poster for the Economic Co-operation Administration, which carried out the Plan. Massive U.S. aid helped Europe to recover from World War Two and enormously increased American influence on European life. Older people often resented the Americanised speech, manners and clothes of the young.

The Welfare State in Britain

▲ **The end of the old British Empire** is described in the chapter called Empires in Retreat. Many people regretted the change and hoped for a closer Commonwealth union to keep Britain among the great powers. The crusader symbol on the masthead of the *Daily Express* was shown in chains as a protest against the supposed neglect of the empire.

Millions had been poor and unemployed before the war. The British people were determined not to let it happen again.

In wartime everyone had a job, and though goods were scarce they were shared out fairly through rationing. In 1942 Sir William Beveridge recommended the idea of a "Welfare State" to protect and help all citizens when the war was over. Some forms of state assistance had existed since the early part of the century, but the Beveridge Report marked the birth of a policy.

All the political parties agreed, but most people felt that the Conservatives were really too attached to the old order. When the first post-war election was held in 1945, a majority voted Labour, even though it meant rejecting the wartime leader Winston Churchill.

Labour quickly set up the Welfare State. A National Insurance scheme arranged regular pay for the unemployed, family allowances for parents of more than one child, and pensions for widows and orphans as well as old people. A National Health Service was introduced, making medical and dental treatment free. And great efforts were made to provide more and better education and housing.

Labour also nationalised public transport, the coal mines and other industries. This meant taking them away from private companies (who were paid compensation) and running them through government-appointed corporations.

The other side of Labour rule was "austerity"—continued rationing, government controls over business, shortages and fuel crises. Paying for the war had put Britain deep into debt, and even with American aid, recovery was painfully slow.

▲ **Nationalisation** was the most controversial of Labour's policies. Supporters argued that industries should be run "on behalf of the people", as this colliery notice proclaims. Opponents pointed out that the actual running was always done by the state, giving still more power to civil servants.

▲ **Free milk at school** was one of the welfare schemes introduced in 1946; the picture shows boys of Manchester Grammar School during a milk-break. Greater concern with children's diet during and after the war led to marked improvements in their health and appearance. Teeth braces and leg irons, once a common sight on the streets, became rare.

▲ **The Festival of Britain, 1951,** displayed the achievements of British science and technology in a complex of splendid new buildings on London's South Bank.

After the Festival

The fifties in Britain were a period of great prosperity—of the kind of "affluence" described on page 42. The Conservatives came back to power and carried out their promise to "set the people free" by ending controls and rationing; but they left untouched the Welfare State set up by Labour.

Although prosperous, Britain was never really secure because she found it hard to sell as much to other countries as she bought from them. Another strain was caused by the effort to remain a great power without the economic strength or the empire of past times. Britain made her own nuclear weapons and spent more on "defence" than most states.

After 1956 it seemed that all the problems could be solved by affluence and "Supermac"— Harold Macmillan, the new prime minister. In fact, by the late fifties Britain was rather complacent.

▲ **Seeking a better life in Britain,** immigrants arrived in large numbers from the West Indies, Pakistan and India. Their different way of life and skin colour made them targets for prejudice, which exploded into the 1958 race riots at Nottingham and London's Notting Hill. Immigrants did not, as some feared, take white people's jobs; they mainly worked in hospitals and transport, which whites would or could not do. But tensions went on into the sixties.

▶ **The coronation of Queen Elizabeth II** in Westminster Abbey. George VI had ruled Britain through the war and the austerity period; people hoped that the new reign would bring prosperity and a new "Elizabethan" greatness. After year-long preparations, the coronation was celebrated with pomp and tremendous popular enthusiasm. The ceremony was watched by millions on television—a fact itself historic.

Indian Independence

The slow winding-up of the British Empire began with the creation of two new states, India and Pakistan.

The vast, teeming land of India had long been "the brightest jewel in the British Crown", but from 1942 British governments were prepared to grant her independence. Many difficulties in doing so were caused by hostilities between the Indians themselves.

The two main religious groups, Hindus and Muslims, distrusted each other. There were far more Hindus, but the Muslims were in a majority in north-west and north-east India. Fearing that they would have no say in a Hindu-dominated government, they demanded that the Muslim areas should become a separate state, "Pakistan".

When all other solutions failed, the British government declared that India would become independent in August 1947—and would have to solve her own problems. It soon became clear that partition was inevitable.

The birth of India and Pakistan was agonising. As independence came nearer, tensions mounted until they exploded in rioting and massacres. Thousands were killed and millions fled—Hindus from Pakistan and Muslims from India. Religious hatred had split the Indian sub-continent in two.

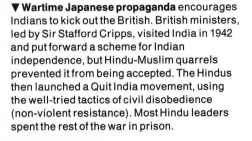

▼ **Wartime Japanese propaganda** encourages Indians to kick out the British. British ministers, led by Sir Stafford Cripps, visited India in 1942 and put forward a scheme for Indian independence, but Hindu-Muslim quarrels prevented it from being accepted. The Hindus then launched a Quit India movement, using the well-tried tactics of civil disobedience (non-violent resistance). Most Hindu leaders spent the rest of the war in prison.

◄**Jawaharlal Nehru** was educated in England at Harrow and Cambridge University, but joined the nationalist movement shortly after his return to India. Though Gandhi was the unchallenged leader of Indian nationalism, Nehru became his right-hand man as president of the Hindu-dominated Nationalist Party Congress. After Independence he became India's first Prime Minister, making his country a leading and influential neutral.

▼ **M. A. Jinnah,** leader of the Muslim League. Jinnah had originally sympathised with the Indian nationalists, but had changed his mind after the provincial elections of 1937, when Congress refused to share power with the Muslim minority. The League's demand for a separate Muslim state was met by the creation of Pakistan. Jinnah was its first Governor General, but his death in 1948 left Pakistan without the strong leadership she needed.

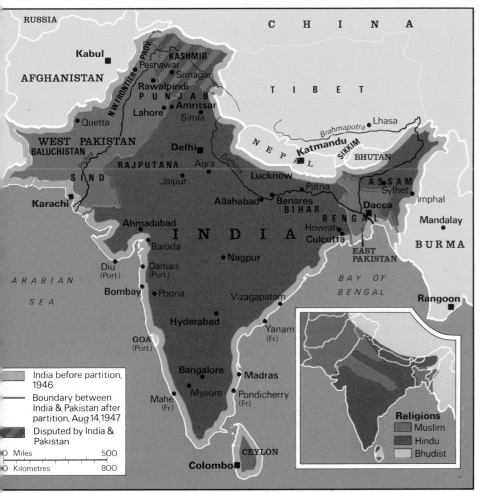

India before partition, 1946

Boundary between India & Pakistan after partition, Aug 14, 1947

Disputed by India & Pakistan

0 Miles 500
0 Kilometres 800

Religions
Muslim
Hindu
Bhudist

▲ **The partition of India** on religious lines created two strangely-shaped countries. In particular, Pakistan consisted of two territories separated by almost a thousand miles. The actual distribution of Hindus and Muslims (see the small map) was even more complicated than the boundary settlements, and led to continual conflict.

Mao in China

The Communist revolution led by Mao Tse-tung gave China a new unity and strength.

▲ **The victorious Red Army** attacking a Nationalist-held town in Manchuria. It was in this wealthy province that the Communists scored their first great post-war successes.

With the defeat of Japan, the wartime alliance between the main Chinese political groups came to an end. Civil war broke out between Chiang Kai shek's Nationalists and the Commu nists led by Mao Tse-tung.

The Nationalists were at first better armed and received much help from the United States. But the Communists had learned effective guerrilla fighting against the Japanese and had seized large quantities of arms when the latter surrendered. In addition, the peasants trusted and aided them. In China Communism seemed to mean libera tion from corrupt landlords and officials

By October 1949 the Communists were strong enough to declare China a People's Republic. By the beginning of 1950 the Nationalists were only holding out on the large island of Taiwan (For mosa), where they were protected by the American fleet. As the United States also used her influence to prevent China from joining the United Nations, the Chinese naturally looked on West ern "imperialism" as her chief enemy.

The other great Communist state, Russia, seemed a firm ally, sending technical experts and equipment to help China build modern industries. The Chinese government took control of existing industries and set about getting rid of the landlords. The peasants were encouraged to join large, jointly-run farms (collective farms) instead of working privately, but this was done less harshly than it had been in Russia.

The striking successes of the early years were followed by some setbacks but most Chinese were better off in Mao's China. The Chinese interven tion in the Korean War (page 24), and her occupation of Tibet in 1950 showed that China was no longer the helpless giant of the previous century but one of the great powers.

◄ **China, ancient and modern.** An old scholar —a follower of the ancient sage Confucius— stands bemused in front of some eager recruits for Mao's Red Army.

Mao Tse-tung in 1943. Mao's enormous prestige in China was based on his leadership of the epic Long March of 1934, and on his part in fighting the Japanese and Chiang Kai-shek. Once in power, he tried to carry out Communist ideals, dividing China into large areas called communes, largely run by the peasants and workers. But Mao's planned industrial expansion—the "Great Leap Forward" of 1958 —overstrained Chinese resources. After this it seemed for some years that Mao's influence had waned.

"Glory to the great Chinese people!" says this 1949 Russian poster celebrating Mao's victory. A Communist China was a tremendous asset to the Communist bloc, and encouraged Communists all over the world. Despite their shared convictions, the Russians had not always helped the Chinese Communists or believed in their chances of victory. But after the Civil War the two countries were firm allies, until the late fifties, when Mao began to suspect Russia of softening in her attitude towards the U.S.A.

▲ **Heroic image of the worker** at China's Da' Ching oilfield. When the Communists took power, China—with the exception of Manchuria—was a poor and backward society of peasants and craftsmen. Industries had to be developed to raise living standards and make China a great power. Although the "Great Leap Forward" was a failure, a degree of industrialisation pushed forward; road and rail communications were improved, and a drive was begun to wipe out illiteracy. This poster reads, "Rely on your own efforts and build up our motherland".

СЛАВА ВЕЛИКОМУ КИТАЙСКОМУ НАРОДУ,
ЗАВОЕВАВШЕМУ СВОБОДУ НЕЗАВИСИМОСТЬ И СЧАСТЬЕ!

The Birth of Israel

Scattered and persecuted for centuries, the Jewish people had never forgotten Israel, their homeland in Biblical times.

In the 1890s a Jewish journalist from Austria, Theodor Herzl, became convinced that the Jews would never be safe until they had a land of their own. Herzl's work led to the Zionist movement, which aimed to resettle Palestine, once the ancient land of Israel.

Progress was slow until 1917, when the British government issued the Balfour Declaration, pledging British support for a Jewish "national home". Then in 1922 Britain was put in charge of Palestine, and a few thousand Jews went there each year. The Arabs felt that their land was being stolen from them and made some savage attacks on Jewish communities.

Later, Nazi persecutions swelled the number of Jews who wanted to take refuge in Palestine. Britain, caught between her promises to the Jews and her need of Arab support, set limits on the number of Jewish immigrants.

Some Jews now turned to terrorism. The killing of British soldiers and civilians in Jerusalem's King David Hotel caused an international stir. The millions of Jewish deaths in concentration camps created a sympathy for Zionism and made Britain unpopular when she turned back ships like the *Exodus*, full of refugees from Europe.

Finally, under pressure from all sides the British tried to hand over to the U.N., which declined to help. In May 1948 the British simply left Palestine. The Jews set up a new state of Israel, defeating the invading armies of Egypt and Transjordan. But the Arabs still declared they would destroy Israel: the Arab-Israeli conflict had ended in a truce, not peace.

▲ **The most notorious Jewish terrorists** were the Stern Gang, shown here on a Wanted poster in Hebrew, put out by the British authorities in 1942.

▼ **Only limited Jewish immigration was allowed** into Palestine from 1939. But many tried—and succeeded—in entering illegally. This is one of the unlucky ones, caught by British troops.

Keeping the Promised Land

Palestine was a British "mandate", which meant that Britain had been put in charge of the country by the League of Nations. When she could no longer control the situation, Britain handed back the mandate to the League's successor, the United Nations.

Dividing Palestine between Jews and Arabs was the solution put forward by the U.N. in 1947. The division (left-hand map) was to include an international zone of great religious importance: Nazareth was the birthplace of Jesus, and Jerusalem is a holy city to Jews, Christians and Muslims. (Most Arabs are Muslims.)

The Arabs rejected the United Nations plan, confident that armies from other Arab states would conquer the whole land once the British went. Their failure left the Israelis holding more territory than the U.N. had proposed (right-hand map).

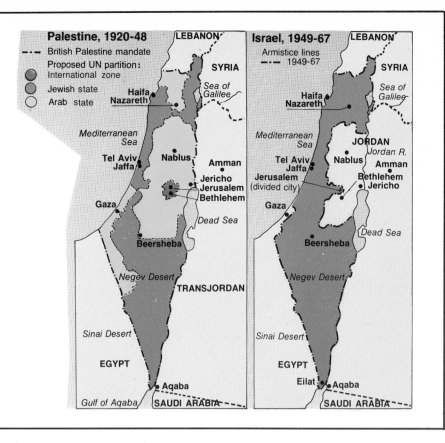

Palestine, 1920-48
- - - British Palestine mandate
Proposed UN partition:
⬤ International zone
⬤ Jewish state
◯ Arab state

LEBANON
SYRIA
Sea of Galilee
Haifa
Nazareth
Mediterranean Sea
Tel Aviv
Jaffa
Nablus
Amman
Jericho
Jerusalem
Bethlehem
Gaza
Dead Sea
Beersheba
Negev Desert
TRANSJORDAN
Sinai Desert
EGYPT
Aqaba
Gulf of Aqaba
SAUDI ARABIA

Israel, 1949-67
Armistice lines
- - - 1949-67

LEBANON
SYRIA
Sea of Galilee
Haifa
Nazareth
Mediterranean Sea
JORDAN
Jordan R.
Tel Aviv
Jaffa
Nablus
Amman
Bethlehem
Jerusalem (divided city)
Jericho
Gaza
Dead Sea
Beersheba
Negev Desert
Sinai Desert
EGYPT
Eilat
Aqaba
SAUDI ARABIA

◀ **Orthodox European Jews find a new life** on the soil of the Promised Land.

▼ **The Palestinian Arabs were the worst sufferers** in the first Arab-Israeli war. Most of them fled in front of the Israeli armies. They were not settled properly in the Arab states they fled to, but herded into camps near the Israeli borders. Their existence made peace in the Middle East highly unlikely.

21

The Suez Crisis

Britain and France had long dominated the Middle East, but the Suez crisis was a victory for the new Arab nationalism and a great jolt to the prestige of the old colonial powers.

▼ **The nine-day crisis.** Israeli armour tore across Sinai on October 29th as paratroops captured the vital Mitla Pass. Britain and France gave Egypt unacceptable terms (October 30th); bombed her (31st); and dropped paratroops on Port Said (November 5th), backed next day by an invasion fleet from Malta. But by then a cease-fire had been arranged.

From the fifties Egypt had a dynamic leader in Abdul Gamal Nasser, who was determined to shake off foreign influence and unite the Arabs in a crusade against Israel.

Nasser's first target was the Suez Canal, a great international waterway that passed through Egypt. The Canal was owned and run by a European company, and down to 1956 it had even been protected by British troops.

These had hardly left Egyptian soil when Nasser quarrelled with the Western powers, who objected to his buying Eastern arms and refused to lend Egypt the money for an important new dam at Aswan. Nasser's reply was dramatic: he announced that Egypt would nationalise the Canal at once.

Most countries disliked this one-sided action but decided to put up with it. Only Britain and France, angry at being tricked into leaving the Canal and fearful for the safety of their oil supplies, looked for an excuse to act. Israel, also menaced by Egypt, was brought in to help: on 29 October 1956 the Israelis launched an all-out attack on Egypt, hammering their way overland towards the Canal.

Britain and France were now able to claim that the fighting threatened international navigation. They demanded that both sides withdraw from the Canal Zone—which of course hit at the Egyptians, who were actually occupying it. And when the Egyptians refused, British and French planes bombed their cities, and a few days later dropped paratroops at Port Said. Egypt seemed doomed.

But world opinion was much more hostile than Britain and France had expected. For once, the Americans and Russians were agreed in denouncing the invasion at the United Nations. Britain ran into money difficulties, and on the day after their arrival the paratroops were ordered to cease firing. A United Nations force took over from them, and the invaders tamely withdrew. It was all over.

For Britain and France, Suez was a fiasco. Their influence was replaced by that of the U.S.A. and Russia, who brought Cold War rivalry into an area already full of dangerous tensions.

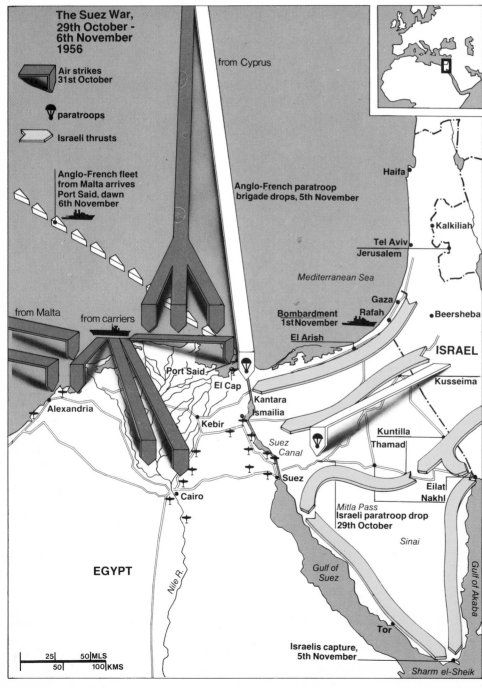

The Suez War, 29th October - 6th November 1956

Air strikes 31st October

paratroops

Israeli thrusts

Anglo-French fleet from Malta arrives Port Said, dawn 6th November

from Cyprus

from Malta

from carriers

Anglo-French paratroop brigade drops, 5th November

Haifa

Kalkiliah

Tel Aviv
Jerusalem

Mediterranean Sea

Gaza
Rafah

Beersheba

Bombardment 1st November

El Arish

ISRAEL

Kusseima

Port Said
El Cap

Kantara
Ismailia

Alexandria

Kebir

Kuntilla
Thamad

Suez Canal

Suez

Cairo

Eilat
Nakhl

Mitla Pass
Israeli paratroop drop 29th October

Sinai

EGYPT

Nile R.

Gulf of Suez

Gulf of Akaba

Tor

Israelis capture, 5th November

Sharm el-Sheik

25   50 MLS
50   100 KMS

▲ **Abdul Nasser** announces the nationalisation of the Canal at Alexandria, 26th July 1956.

▶ **Egyptian and Russian workers on the Aswan Dam.** The Suez crisis gave the Russians a chance to help—and influence—the Arabs.

▲**Israeli soldier with Egyptian prisoners.** Constantly threatened by the Arabs and refused navigation rights through the Canal or in the Gulf of Akaba, Israel willingly joined Britain and France. She, at least, gained something from Suez—freedom of navigation in the Gulf.

◀ **British lion and French cock humiliated** by the Egyptian sphinx. It was not really Egypt that defeated the Anglo-French expedition (as this Russian cartoon implies) but American economic pressure, world opinion, and perhaps the threats of the Russians themselves.

23

War in Korea

▲ **General MacArthur and Syngman Rhee:**
U.N. commander and South Korean president.

In the "hottest" event of the Cold War, the United States repulsed Communist aggression without risking a World War.

In 1950 there were two Korean states divided by an imaginary geographical line, the 38th parallel. Communist North Korea had been set up by the Russians, and South Korea by the Americans. Each claimed to be the true government of all Korea, and there were constant border clashes.

In June 1950 eight well-equipped North Korean divisions suddenly launched a surprise attack on the poorly armed South. Within a few days the United Nations condemned North Korea as an aggressor, and a U.N. force was organized to help the South. Most of the force was supplied by the United States, but fourteen other nations also took part.

The North Koreans were no match for the U.S. Army, which was soon nearing the boundary between North Korea and China. But now the Chinese,
alarmed by the approach of U.S. troops, entered the war by sending "volunteers" to help North Korea.

This could have been the start of a world war. The U.N. commander, General MacArthur, argued that victory could only be won by attacking China herself. President Truman thought it wiser to limit the war to Korea. When MacArthur, a popular hero of World War Two, publicly disagreed, Truman firmly dismissed him.

Events proved Truman was right. The war ended in a stalemate, roughly along the line of the original boundary, the 38th parallel. Peace talks went on from 1951, and an armistice was finally signed in July 1953.

▼ **Civilians suffered terribly** in the war, as in all modern wars. A million are said to have died, and many more became homeless refugees.

Lockheed Shooting Star XP-80A, a jet fighter capable of flying at 558 m.p.h. and dropping ,000 lbs of bombs. It was the most advanced et plane produced during World War Two, but did not in fact see combat until Korea.

The Korean War gave both sides in the Cold War the chance to try out new weapons. It was the first war in which jets fought each other face to face, in dogfights at incredible speeds.

The U.S. Shooting Stars and Sabres had a marked superiority over the Russian MIGs used by the Chinese and North Koreans. But, as in the World War, heavy bombing was less successful than expected in destroying enemy industries and lines of communication.

The Korean War

Blue arrows—North Korean advance
Red arrows—U.N. lines

◀ **In the first phase of the war,** North Korea attacked the South and the United Nations intervened. Although they claimed that the South started the war, the North Koreans attacked in overwhelming force (1). They pushed back the South Koreans and the first U.S. troops to a small area round Pusan (2). But they were unable to wipe out this pocket, which U.N. forces poured into. A brilliant flank attack by U.S. marines at Inchon (3) led to the collapse of the Communist army (4) and a rapid advance into the North (5). By November 24th the U.N. seemed about to finish off the enemy (6).

▶ **The war was transformed** on 26th November when two large armies of Chinese "volunteers" appeared in North Korea and pushed back the U.N. forces (7). The pretence that the armies had not been sent by the Chinese government meant that there need not be an all-out war between China and the U.S.A. and her allies. The Chinese drove the U.N. out of North Korea and even penetrated into the South (8). Then a reinforced U.N. beat off fresh attacks and advanced again, inflicting huge casualties on the Chinese. U.N. troops finally dug in along the "Kansas-Wyoming" Line (9), the eventual armistice line.

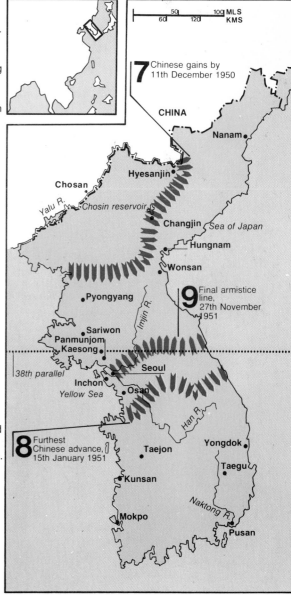

From Stalin to Khrushchev

Stalin dominated Russia for nearly thirty years. His death began a movement for greater freedom under Communism.

Stalin was widely admired for leading Russia to victory in the war and making her a great industrial power. But he was also a ruthless dictator, insanely suspicious even of other Communists. Secret police were everywhere, and millions of people were sentenced to slave labour.

After Stalin's death in 1953, conditions gradually improved. The secret police were controlled and many prisoners were released.

By 1955 Nikita Khrushchev had emerged as the new Soviet leader. A year later he made a famous speech denouncing Stalin's crimes. Although many Communists were disillusioned by what they heard, Khrushchev's speech seemed to promise more changes and a better life under Communism.

The first effects were felt inside the "satellites", the East European states ruled by followers of Stalin. In 1953 East German riots had been crushed. But in the new atmosphere of 1956 the Russians accepted Polish demands for a "National" Communism—run in their own interests.

This was as far as the Russians would go. In November 1956, a similar movement in Hungary turned into an anti-Communist revolution. Soviet tanks moved into Budapest, pounding much of the city to rubble and killing thousands of people. Communism remained a compulsory way of life.

▲ **Thirty years of Soviet power** are celebrated on this anniversary poster. It also praises the Russian peasantry and the collective farm system, though in fact agriculture was the least successful part of the Soviet economy. Communist propaganda of this sort told the workers that they ran Russia, but the reality was different.

▶ **Hungarian rebels** gather round their national flag. Most East Europeans resented Russian domination even more than Communist dictatorship. But while Poland settled for a Polish brand of Communism under Wladislaw Gomulka, the Hungarian prime minister, Imre Nagy, promised free elections (which might have meant the end of Communist rule) and announced Hungarian neutrality in the Cold War. At this point Russia sent in her tanks.

Khrushchev's visit to Yugoslavia in 1955 was an attempt to restore good relations with the rebel Communist state. Yugoslavia's Marshall Tito (left) listened to Khrushchev's apologies but continued his policy of neutrality in the Cold War. Khrushchev was prepared to allow East European countries more independence—provided they remained in the Communist camp.

▼ **The "personality cult" of Stalin** pictured him as the all-wise leader and teacher. Here he is receiving the thanks of Russian children for their happy childhood. Millions of people did idolise Stalin, both inside and outside Russia. Even after Khrushchev's speech, some Communist countries such as Albania and China remained determinedly "Stalinist".

Sport and Adventure

With the end of the war, sport again became universally popular and increasingly professionalised.

▲ **The 1948 Olympic Games** in London were a sign that sporting competition was returning to normal. Captain Willy Grut of the Swedish Army (centre) won the Modern Pentathlon.

There was little time or money for sports during the war, and international competition stopped almost altogether. Young men and women were occupied with wartime duties, and rationing and other hardships had their effect.

Not surprisingly, new talents were slow to come forward, and many post-war sports were still dominated by heroes of the thirties. Such were the Australian cricketer Don Bradman, the U.S. heavyweight boxer Joe Louis, the British golfer Henry Cotton, and the champion jockey Gordon Richards.

The new players who emerged in the fifties tended to be younger than ever before. Teenagers like "Little Mo"— tennis champion Maureen Connolly— beat older and more experienced players with apparent ease.

One reason was the training had become more scientific, so that players reached an early peak of skill and fitness. This also meant that amateurs had little chance of competing successfully with professionals. And in fact, many "amateurs" in sports like tennis and athletics were full-time players who had been given easy jobs and good training facilities by large organisations or, in Communist countries, governments.

The new trends were often deplored, but they made the post-war period one of the great ages of record-breaking.

Motor Racing

▲ **The Maserati 250F** was one of the great racing cars of the fifties. It won the first race for which it was entered, the 1954 Argentine Grand Prix. In 1957 the outstanding driver of the period, Juan Fangio, won the world championship— for the fifth time—driving a 254. He retired in the following year.

◀ **Stirling Moss** at the wheel of his car at Silverstone racing track. Moss was a popular personality in British racing during the fifties, and was national champion every year except 1953. Another British driver, Mike Hawthorne, won the world championship in 1958, paving the way for the many British triumphs of the sixties.

High Seas Adventure

Adventures are still possible in the modern world. One of the most exciting took place in 1947, when the raft *Kon-Tiki* sailed 4,000 miles from South America to the Tuamotu Islands in the Pacific. The leader of the expedition, a Norwegian scholar called Thor Heyerdahl, wanted to prove that the American Indians could have settled the Pacific islands. The six-man crew had to live on what they could find or catch in the ocean—including sharks.

Mountaineering made news in 1953, when Everest, the world's highest peak, was conquered by a British expedition. The two men who reached the top were a New Zealander, Edmund Hillary, and his Nepalese guide, Tenzing. Hillary was knighted by Queen Elizabeth and later led the New Zealand group in another adventure of the fifties, the Commonwealth trans-Antarctic expedition.

▶ **The Kon-Tiki raft** was made of balsa wood logs lashed together with hemp—the only materials the South Americans could have used to make the trip across the Pacific.

▲ **British Roger Bannister,** running his 3 m. 59.4 sec. mile at Oxford, May 6, 1954. Breaking the nine-year-old record set by Gunder Hägg was almost incidental to his triumphant assault on the generally-held belief that the under 4 minute mile was impossible.

▼ **The World Cup,** staged every four years, is the premier trophy of football. Uruguay won it in 1950, West Germany in 1954, Brazil in 1958.

The rise of continental and South American teams was a striking feature of the fifties. All traces of the old English supremacy vanished with World Cup losses to Brazil and Spain in 1950. This was confirmed in 1953, when England suffered her first-ever home loss at Wembley, (6-3 to the Hungarians, captained by Puskas, below).

Fad and Fashion

Fashions after the war changed as quickly as ever. One new feature was clothing made especially for young people.

▲ **The middle-class male,** dressed in traditionally quiet style. This is a smart model version of the cardigan and baggy trousers worn by many men at home after a day spent in a dark business suit.

Wartime clothing was drab. Rationing stopped people from buying much, and special "utility" clothes were made, using as little material as possible. So short skirts were favoured, and the pre-war square-shouldered look carried on unchanged. The only hints of luxury were the long hair, and occasionally the silk stockings, worn by women.

By 1947 the French fashion designer Christian Dior had introduced the "New Look" in rebellion against wartime styles. Its keynotes were femininity and extravagance: quantities of material were used, curves were emphasised, and long full skirts were made with many pleats and gathers.

In the fifties the main trend was towards simplicity and casualness,

though the Paris fashion houses still wielded great influence. Sweaters and cardigans were worn for much of the time by both men and women, and young people often adopted the jeans and duffle coat popularised by students. Man-made materials such as nylon, terylene and tricel made it cheaper and easier for ordinary people to dress smartly.

The advantage of "student" styles was their cheapness. But many young people were earning high wages and could afford quite expensive clothes. The "Teddy Boys" (see below) were the first of many teenage groups to dress —and behave—with the rebellious independence of the adult world. A teenage sub-culture was born.

▲ **Teddy Boys,** with their long draped jackets, "drainpipe" trousers, crepe-soled shoes and lavishly oiled hair. Adults generally resented them, and they got a bad name as a result of some gang fights and riots in cinemas.

▶ **Jiving in gingham.** The bright, simple frock, big belt and nipped waist are typical of the styles favoured by young people who could not afford *haute couture* (high fashion) clothes like those at the top of the next page.

▲ **Models of 1946,** showing off the full-skirted post-war look, with its rather dumpy hats and wide lapels.

▲ **The 1949 Paris look,** designed for the rich and smart, with nipped waist, lower hemline and higher heels.

▲ **The sheath dress, 1954,** worn with a close-fitting turban. Its simpler lines meant it was much easier to mass-produce.

The bikini was one of the sensations of the fifties. In the twenties there had been an uproar over one-piece bathing suits that showed girls' legs. Now the bikini, revealing the midriff and navel, was attacked in the same way; in some of the less tolerant Mediterranean countries the girls who wore it were likely to be arrested. But, as in the twenties, the new style soon came to be accepted by everyone.

▶ **The sack** was one of several similar dress styles appearing in the late fifties; others were the sheath, shown above, and the rather fuller, more tent-like trapeze dress. They were typical of the period in their simple lines and sparing use of accessories. Combined with a long bead necklace, the sack might easily have passed as a style of the twenties. But both the blonde and the pose she is striking are very much of the fifties.

The Dawn of the Nuclear Age

"The Bomb" was the nightmare of the forties and fifties. Yet nuclear energy could also be used to benefit humanity.

The terrible atomic bombs that destroyed Hiroshima and Nagasaki took their force from nuclear energy—the immense power released as the result of a nuclear chain reaction.

The destruction of cities in a few moments changed everybody's ideas about war—especially as ownership of "the Bomb" spread. In 1945 only the U.S.A. had it, but the U.S.S.R. joined the "nuclear club" in 1949 and Britain followed in 1952. All three then pressed on to make thermo-nuclear weapons—hydrogen bombs—with even greater destructive power.

As bombs and later missiles (rockets carrying nuclear "warheads") piled up, it began to seem likely that a war would destroy the human race. There were also dangers caused by the need to test new types of nuclear weapon. Every explosion left "fall-out", a cloud of radioactive dust that spread through the Earth's atmosphere, poisoning it.

Such horrors caused protests in many countries. Disarmament talks made no progress, but in 1958 the three nuclear powers did at least agree to stop testing their weapons.

The energy that destroyed cities could also be used peacefully as a form of power, like electricity. Nuclear power could replace the Earth's coal and oil, which were rapidly being used up. A beginning was made in the fifties, when the first nuclear power stations and nuclear-powered ships were built.

Radioactivity too was harnessed to the needs of science and medicine.

▲ **Beautiful but deadly:** H-bomb blast at Bikini Atoll in the Pacific, 1956.

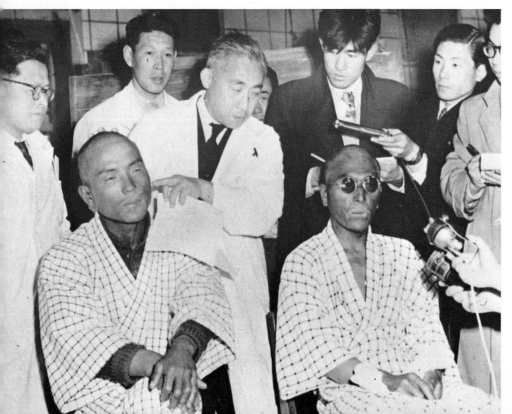

◀ **Victims of fallout** being shown to reporters by a doctor. The victims were two of the twenty-three crewmen of a Japanese fishing boat, the Lucky Dragon. The boat was caught in a shower of poisonous radioactive dust from the U.S. H-bomb test at Bikini Atoll in March 1954. The whole crew was badly burned and one member later died in hospital. Though widely publicised, the accident did not lead to the end of testing.

◀ **Protest** was aroused by nuclear tests, as in this 1957 student rally held outside the British embassy at Tokyo. But some groups were opposed to the very idea of a country having nuclear weapons. In Britain, for example, the Campaign for Nuclear Disarmament (C.N.D.) marched every year from London to Aldermaston, a centre of atomic weapons research, to persuade British governments to ''Ban the Bomb''.

▼ **Calder Hall,** Britain's first atomic power station, being opened by Queen Elizabeth on 17th October 1956. Atomic submarines had already been built, as well as bombs, but Calder Hall was the first use of nuclear energy for ordinary peacetime purposes. Thanks to pioneering work at Harwell and Hinton, Britain remained ahead of both the U.S.A. and U.S.S.R. in this field. Much of her electricity was soon generated by nuclear power.

Films of the Fifties

▲ **Ashes and Diamonds** is a brilliant Polish film made by Andrzej Wajda in 1958. It shows people caught up in the rivalries of Polish politics after the war. In most Communist films life was seen in over-simple terms, with Communists always heroes. But more freedom of thought was allowed in Poland, and film-makers could show the confused course of real life.

▼ **Hollywood musicals** were as lively and tuneful as ever, but like other American films they grew longer and more spectacular in the fifties. In musicals like this one (*Oklahoma!*) the outdoor setting and homely characters made a refreshing change from stories about starlets or princes or sailors, though they were actually no more realistic than before.

Film-making became an international industry in the fifties; Hollywood's supremacy ended but films were probably better

The cinema achieved its peak popularity just after the war, when millions of people went each week. In the fifties audiences were smaller; people who owned television sets were less and less willing to go out to see run-of-the-mill films.

Hollywood's answer was to make fewer but longer and more spectacular, star-studded films, shown in colour on giant screens. By the late fifties "epics" such as *Ben-Hur* were taking years to make and were being shot on location— in real settings instead of in Hollywood studios. So Hollywood stopped being the world's "film capital", though American stars, directors and producers remained as important as ever.

For the first time, films made in Europe and Asia became internationally famous. Italy, Sweden and Poland had flourishing film industries, and directors like Satyajit Ray and Kurosawa aroused interest in the Indian and Japanese cinema. Many of the new European films had the kind of difficult style found in modern art, especially after the appearance of the French "New Wave" films from 1958.

Ducks and geese and chicks gonna scurry, when I take you out in the surrey, When I take you out in the surrey with the fringe on top.

▶ **Natural Vision** was one of the ''3-D'' (three-dimensional) processes introduced in the fifties. 3-D films gave a lifelike appearance of space and distance—so much so that audiences ducked when a lion jumped in their direction. But 3-D never became widely popular, nor did the giant screen of Cinerama. Both were attempts to make the big screen more interesting and win back lost audiences. CinemaScope and other ''wide-screen'' processes were more successful. Combined with colour, they were used for most big U.S. films.

▼ **Marilyn Monroe** in *There's No Business Like Show Business* (1954). Monroe's sex appeal and enchanting personality made her the pin-up of the fifties, hiding her considerable dramatic talent.

▲ **La Strada** (*The Road*, 1954) gave the Italian director Federico Fellini an international reputation. The stars, Fellini's wife Giulietta Masina and American actor Anthony Quinn, play two buskers; Masina, as Quinn's much-abused helper, is wonderfully funny and touching. Post-war Italian cinema had been known for its realism, but directors like Fellini and Michelangelo Antonioni made more personal films with a strong element of fantasy.

▲ **The Knight plays chess with Death** in this scene from *The Seventh Seal* (1956). If the Knight wins, Death will spare him—but Death is an unbeatable master. The film is set in plague-stricken Sweden during the Middle Ages, but its harrowing view of life is typical of the Swedish director Ingmar Bergman. Many people sympathised with the despair of his characters, who have lost all belief in God and human progress.

The United States: Pride and Prejudice

American supremacy continued into the fifties, but Americans became more anxious about threats to their way of life.

▲ **General Eisenhower** (right) and Richard M. Nixon in 1952, shortly after their nomination as Republican Party candidates for president and vice-president. Eisenhower was elected and was in office for the rest of the fifties; Nixon had a long, stormy career ahead of him.

Harry S. Truman remained U.S. president until 1952. His foreign policy was strong, but at home Congress refused to pass many of the "Fair Deal" laws he wanted. His successor was Dwight D. Eisenhower, who had won tremendous popularity as the wartime commander of the Allied armies in western Europe.

The Eisenhower era (1952-60) was one of cautious, conservative government; the United States was growing still wealthier, and most Americans did not want drastic changes or experiments.

The only threat to their power and prosperity, they felt, was Communism —which meant Russia and China abroad and spies and Communists in the U.S. In a sensational spy trial Ethel and Julius Rosenberg were found guilty of giving atomic secrets to Russia; many believed they were innocent, but they were executed in 1953.

The U.S. Communist Party was outlawed and the beliefs of government employees were investigated. Then the "witch-hunt" spread to jobs that had nothing to do with politics. Anti-Communism became a way of getting on in U.S. politics, and Senator Joe McCarthy gained considerable power by making wild accusations against government and army leaders. "McCarthyism" was only discredited in 1954, when the senator went too far; but fear of Communism continued to exert a powerful influence on the popular mind.

In the late fifties there were signs of change. American economic troubles and Russian space achievements indicated that U.S. supremacy might not last forever; and a visit to the U.S.A. by the Russian leader Khrushchev suggested that the Cold War might at last be coming to an end.

◄ **America's happy and prosperous people,** united in love of country. That is how this trucking advertisement pictured Americans, and is probably how most of them saw themselves in the fifties.

▲ **Violence at a Hollywood strike.** The "dream factory" showed America as its most glamorous, but Hollywood was in fact a centre of labour trouble and anti-Communist persecution. "Communist" film people were imprisoned or "blacklisted" to stop them working.

◄ **Violence in books and comics** was often blamed for the violence in American life. Murder was far more common than in other Western countries, and teenage crime increased steadily. The cartoon here is Russian, but it reflects the feelings of many Americans.

Elizabeth Eckford, one of nine negro students who tried to take their places at the Central High School, Little Rock. State troops kept them out until Eisenhower sent in Federal troops.

The Fight for Rights

The Civil Rights Movement aimed to make negroes full citizens of the U.S.A. They were supposed to have the same rights as white people, but in the southern states where most negroes lived, whites controlled the state governments. Negro voting rights, though they existed in law, were often denied, and negroes were only allowed in the backs of buses and did not study at the same schools as whites.

This separation—called "segregation"—meant in practice that negroes got worse buses and schools than whites. And bad schooling kept negroes poor and ignorant, so that they also had worse jobs and houses.

The first Civil Rights victories came when negroes boycotted some segregated buses and the U.S. Supreme Court declared segregation unconstitutional (1954). But this and various Civil Rights laws made in Washington were largely ignored by state governments. In 1957, at Little Rock in Arkansas, only troops sent by the President ensured that negro students were admitted to High School.

Civil Rights supporters continued to march and demonstrate, led by Martin Luther King. But progress was so slow that some began to question his peaceful methods.

Peron in Argentina

The most glamorous figures in turbulent South America were Juan Peron, dictator of Argentina, and his beautiful wife Eva.

Central and South America—"Latin" America—was a highly unstable area. Most Latin American states changed their system of government every few years, and the army often interfered in politics to depose a president or set up a military dictatorship.

In the fifties, oil-rich Venezuela, for example, was ruled by the military government of Jiminez; Cuba and Santo Domingo (the Dominican Republic) suffered under dictators who had ruled them since the thirties.

The outstanding democratic government was Brazil's. Under President Kubitschek (1955-64), considerable economic progress was made and by 1959, a splendid new capital city, Brasilia, was under construction.

Argentina was also a large and relatively prosperous country. It was ruled by an army government from 1943 to 1946, when a free election was held and General Juan Peron became president.

Peron had been a popular minister of labour in the military government, and as president he made the workers and their trade unions the basis of his power. Wages were kept high, banks and railways were nationalised, and women were given the vote.

As a result, Peron won the 1951 election easily, and began to change Argentina into a one-party dictatorship.

But then everything seemed to go wrong. Peron's popular wage policies had been possible because of Argentina's prosperity, which now began to waver. Prices rose steeply. Peron's wife Eva, a popular idol, died. The government quarrelled with the Church. Finally, alarmed by a rumour that Peron intended to arm his supporters, the army and navy revolted and overthrew Peron and Peronism.

▲ **Eva Peron,** an ex-actress, was also a politician of real ability. In 1945 she organised huge demonstrations that saved the political career of Juan Peron, who had not yet become her husband. Later her glamour and clever handling of Argentina's women helped to sustain Peron's dictatorship. Her death in 1952 caused nation-wide mourning and weakened the regime.

▲ **Crowds celebrate Peron's fall,** tearing down posters and burning them. In spite of the celebrations, support for Peron remained strong for almost twenty years, especially among trade unionists. Peron was finally recalled from exile and again became president a few months before his death in 1974.

▶ **Peronist propaganda.** A mock cinema poster attacks the slick characters who spend their time gambling and drinking. Peron is quoted as saying that people who do not work are parasites living on those who do. The message is emphasised by the workers in the background who are thronging into the factories—the "New Argentina".

Rock n' Roll

♦ Two images of Pop. Buddy Holly (above) looked the clean-cut American boy and sang harmless songs of teenage love. The darkly handsome Elvis Presley (below) seemed wilder, sexier, more delinquent, though films like *Jailhouse Rock* were basically sentimental.

Rock n' Roll was a dynamic new kind of music that took the West by storm in the late fifties.

Until then, the most typical popular music had been sentimental ballads sung by "crooners" such as Bing Crosby and Frank Sinatra.

Then in 1954 Bill Haley and his Comets made the first really popular Rock 'n' Roll records: *Shake, Rattle and Roll* and *Rock Around the Clock*—cheerful, noisy numbers with a fast, pounding beat. They topped record charts all over America and Europe, and began the Rock craze.

Rock was not strictly new, since it was based on Rhythm 'n' Blues, a kind of Negro music popular in the American South. Its hectic rhythms and enormously amplified electric guitars were the basis of Rock 'n' Roll, and many of the best Rock performers were Southerners such as Jerry Lee Lewis and Little Richard.

Europe also took up Rock 'n' Roll, producing stars like Cliff Richard and Billy Fury in England, and Johnny Halliday in France.

Rock was above all the music of the young. Teenagers were beginning to think of themselves as a separate group, different from adults. With affluence they had money to spend, and more and more records were made specially for the teenage market. The words were still often sentimental ("Why must I be a teenager in love?") but some singers—notably "the King", Elvis Presley—introduced an atmosphere of sex and rebellion which was to start a Pop revolution.

▲ **Fanclubs** became bigger than ever with the boom in popular music of all kinds. Here the idol is the ultra-sentimental pianist Liberace.

◀ **Lively and energetic** to match Rock 'n' Roll, jiving became more popular than conventional "ballroom" dances like the foxtrot.

▼ **Young, moody and rebellious,** like the songs of the fifties: the film star James Dean, whose death on his motor cycle made him a cult hero.

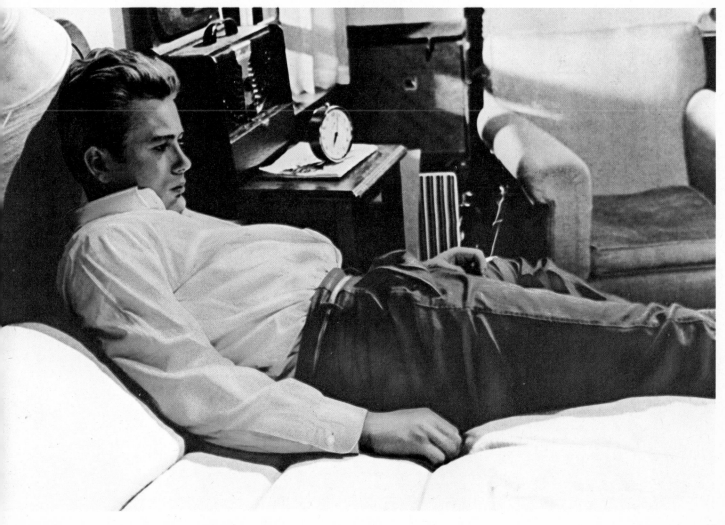

The Affluent Society

By the late fifties the war was becoming a memory. In many industrialised countries people were enjoying a standard of living higher than ever before.

▲ **Japanese girls in a toy factory.** Japan had been an industrialised country before the war, and with U.S. help she recovered from it quickly. By the late fifties she was producing large numbers of ships, electronic goods such as transistors, and cars.

Europe experienced the kind of boom that had made the United States the first "affluent society". The Germans performed an "economic miracle", and in Britain the prime minister, Harold Macmillan, told the people they had "never had it so good".

"Affluence" meant more than just prosperity: it meant that the mass of ordinary people could afford things that had always been regarded as luxuries for the rich. Cars and television sets became common among all classes, and so did labour-saving devices such as vacuum cleaners, refrigerators and washing machines.

Labour-saving was also an advantage of launderettes, and of supermarkets selling a growing range of tinned and frozen foods. Labour-saving meant that people had more leisure time as well as more money, and entertainments boomed. Coffee bars, restaurants, bingo halls, bowling alleys and musical shows attracted crowds; enjoyment of popular music led to big sales of records, transistor radios and tape recorders.

Business and industry wanted people to keep on buying. One way of encouraging them was hire purchase, which allowed the customer to take away goods and pay for them later in instalments. Another way was to persuade people by effective advertising and attractive packaging.

Advertising was sometimes attacked for giving exaggerated and distorted pictures of life. Another drawback of affluence was "built-in obsolescence", which means making goods that soon break or become out of date—so that the owner will keep on buying. But in the fifties these things seemed a small price to pay for the blessings of affluence.

▲ **Air travel** remained a luxury, but one that people could now afford for a once-a-year holiday. By air they could go faster and further, to foreign places instead of local seaside resorts. Most people had never travelled abroad except on war service, but in the fifties tourism became big business. Holiday camps and organised group holidays kept costs low and made a friendly setting in which people could get used to foreign ways.

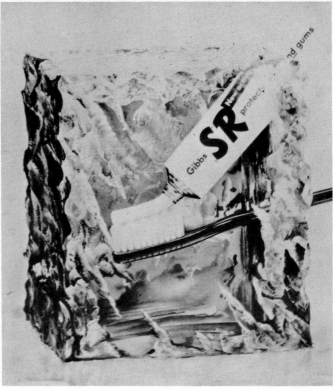

▲ **T.V. commercials** brought a persuasive form of advertising into the home. The toothpaste-in-ice advertisement was the first one shown on British television (22nd September 1955). The plastic ice cleverly suggests that the toothpaste is fresh and clean.

◀**The advertiser's ideal** was the well-dressed, well-groomed, big-spending couple like this one from a *Life* magazine of 1955. Such advertisers were often accused of encouraging people to believe that glamour and goods brought happiness.

▼ **A supermarket** is a large store carrying a very wide range of goods; instead of asking an assistant for what they want, customers walk round with baskets and serve themselves. Supermarkets began in the U.S.A., but in the fifties they spread all over western Europe (the one shown is French). Shoppers could take their time and get what they wanted under one roof; at the same time, the bigger size of supermarkets and the saving in assistants' wages made goods cheaper.

▲ **B.B.C. television announcers, 1950.** T.V. in Europe had to begin again from scratch after the war. By 1959 there were 36 million American sets; Britain had produced 10 million, while France and Germany were going forward rather slowly, with about 2 million each.

Cars

The "family car" that ordinary people could afford had been planned in the thirties, but never developed because of the war. By the fifties the age of mass motoring had arrived at last

▲ **Motor cycles** were glamorised by one of the most popular film stars, Marlon Brando, in *The Wild One*. Dramatically leather-clad, he had a kind of tough rebelliousness that many teenagers admired. Gangs of motor cyclists sometimes behaved anti-socially—not so much through hooliganism as through the cult of driving at recklessly high speeds.

Mass production, cheapness and efficiency could best be achieved by a few really large firms in which all the processes were highly mechanised. In the U.S.A., the car industry had been dominated by such firms since the twenties. Now the same trend was seen in Europe.

It was most marked in Britain, where Morris absorbed famous firms like Riley, Wolseley and M.G., and then merged with Austin to form B.M.C. (the British Motor Corporation). Rootes was another expanding company, taking over Humber, Hillman, Singer and Sunbeam Talbot. The new owners kept many of the old names, but usually the cars produced were only variations on a single style.

This standardisation had its advantages, especially in keeping costs low. Remarkably cheap family cars were made—small, compact, sturdy, quite comfortable and yet with ample room for luggage. Millions of people became car owners for the first time, often with the help of hire purchase. The most popular of the small cars were those produced by the German Volkswagen, the French Citröen and Renault, the Italian Fiat, and the British Morris companies.

Even America was affected by the development of the family car. Seven of the ten million cars produced each year were made in the U.S.A. Most of them were as wide and long as ever, and increasingly low-slung and streamlined. But a section of the American market did start buying the more economical European models. As a result, U.S. manufacturers soon added compact and sports cars to their range, stimulating the growth of the "two-car family".

▲ **Traffic jams** on the way to the seaside. Once motoring stopped being a luxury, this became a familiar holiday sight. Choked city centres were a yet more serious problem.

▲ **A car on the beach** became one of the most popular images of luxury and leisure. The car was more than a useful means of transport—it was a "status symbol" used to show off the class or wealth of the owner. "Keeping up with the Joneses"—that is, with the neighbours—was an attitude encouraged by affluence (see page 42), and applied above all to cars.

▲ **Fatal accidents** were a tragic result of more crowded roads. The British "Keep Death off the Road" series of posters tried to bring home the dangers of carelessness.

◄ **Volkswagen emblem** made up of dozens of the popular "Beetles". In 1972 Volkswagen was to be the world's best-selling car.

1949 Buick, a big, powerful American car, very showy with its sleek lines and lavish chrome. It certainly reflected American wealth and desire for display, but larger cars and bigger engines were also needed for motoring on the vast American continent.

◄ **1956 Austin A40,** a British "family car", very much more modest than the Buick. It was cheaper, more economical in petrol consumption and more compact for parking in Britain's crowded cities. Its severe lines look like a deliberate rejection of luxury appeal.

The Arts

Western post-war arts were widely appreciated and well supported; every kind of experiment was encouraged. But in the arts themselves there was a mood of anxiety and despair.

▲ **Jean-Paul Sartre,** the French existentialist philosopher; also a playwright and novelist of great power.

▼ **Animal Farm** satirises Communist Russia in farmyard terms. This is a still from the film made out of George Orwell's book.

The outstanding new writers of the forties were the French "existentialists", Jean-Paul Sartre and Albert Camus. The experience of the wartime Resistance Movement can be seen in much of their work, which deals with moral choice and the search for meaning. In Italy, Alberto Moravia combined mastery as a storyteller with a deep understanding of human nature.

In the United States the mood was more confident. The first truly American style of painting emerged: Abstract Expressionism. Painters such as Mark Rothko and Jackson Pollock put on colours freely, with no preconceived pattern in mind. They used a brush or knife, or dribbled or threw the paint on ("action painting").

Modern art was no longer merely a subject for laughter. Now experiment was admired and encouraged; composers wrote music for electronic devices, while sculptors exhibited crushed car bodies as their work.

With affluence there was more money to spend on the arts. Big organisations commissioned architects and painters to work for them. The public bought more books and supported the theatre, opera and ballet. And, thanks to government and private grants, art festivals became common.

In spite of all this, the mood of most art was pessimistic. Artists reacted to the horror of Nazi concentration camps, the terrible new weapons, the loss of religious faith. Samuel Beckett wrote novels and plays full of despair. The sculptor Alberto Giacometti created strange, anxious little figures. And Francis Bacon painted men and women with the distorted faces of victims.

The literary event of the fifties was Boris Pasternak's *Dr Zhivago*, a novel which proved that there were still independent spirits in rigid Communist Russia.

▲ **The Sadler's Wells Ballet.** Margot Fonteyn and Michael Somes in *Sylvia*. This London company, founded in 1946, was largely responsible for the postwar popularity of ballet in England. It was renamed the Royal Ballet in 1957.

► **The faceless man,** alone in an empty world. A painful view of life, typical of the Irish painter Francis Bacon.

▼ **The convent of Notre-Dame du Haut,** Ronchamp, was designed by the great Swiss architect Le Corbusier in 1955. Before the war Le Corbusier pioneered the austere straight-lined "modern style".

Empires in Retreat

In 1945 huge areas of Asia and Africa were still ruled by European powers. But the post-war period was one of rapid "decolonisation", creating many new independent countries.

▼ **"The Indies must be free"**, says this anti-Japanese poster issued by the Dutch. But many natives of the Dutch East Indies saw the Japanese as liberators, and in any case did not want the Dutch back. Sukarno, the nationalist leader, was able to build up a strong movement under Japanese rule, and set up an Indonesian republic immediately after the war ended.

At the end of the war France left Syria and Lebanon, and the colonies of wartime enemies—ex-Italian Libya and ex-Japanese Korea—were put on the road to independence.

The Dutch East Indies, which had been occupied by Japan, set up the republic of Indonesia—a scattered group of islands on the map, but in fact a large country with a population of 80 million. The Dutch could neither subdue the Indonesians nor persuade them into partnership.

Most colonial powers tried to keep links with their ex-colonies. Easily the most successful attempt was the British Commonwealth—probably because Britain had been more willing than most to grant self-government.

In 1945 the Commonwealth consisted of countries mainly settled by Europeans, such as Canada and Australia. But the next few years showed that other peoples could be brought into it. By 1959 India, Pakistan, Ceylon, Malaya and Ghana had all become independent and members of the Commonwealth. Central African and West Indian Federations were among other British moves to dismantle this largest of all colonial empires.

But the process was not always smooth. Britain got into difficulties in Palestine, had to put down Communist guerillas in Malaya, and faced hostility in Cyprus and Kenya. In the Middle East, where Britain wanted to remain strong, her influence weakened steadily and ended for good with the Suez fiasco (page 22).

The French were quite determined to keep their empire, though this policy proved disastrous. In Indo-China they were resisted by Communist guerrillas in a long and exhausting war that lasted until 1957 and ended in a humiliating defeat for France.

Within months France was faced with a new rebellion—in Algeria, the most important part of France's vast North African empire. Eventually the Algerian problem caused a crisis in France itself which brought the wartime leader General de Gaulle back into power. It soon became clear that French rule in North Africa was also near its end.

The battle of Dien Bien Phu was the climax of a seven-year war in the French colony of Indo-China. The French army was confident that it could always defeat the rebel guerrillas—the Communist Viet Minh —in open warfare. But when French parachutists occupied Dien Bien Phu, a village deep in Viet Minh territory, it was soon in the grip of a 167-day siege. The heroism of the 13,000 French defenders proved useless. They were ceaselessly pounded by guns on the surrounding hills, and in May 1954 waves of fanatical Viet Minh finally overwhelmed them.

After this crushing defeat France hurriedly withdrew from Indo-China, which was then divided between Communist and non-Communist states. The lesson of the war—repeated in Algeria and elsewhere— was that well-equipped modern armies could be outwitted and utterly demoralised by dedicated guerrillas.

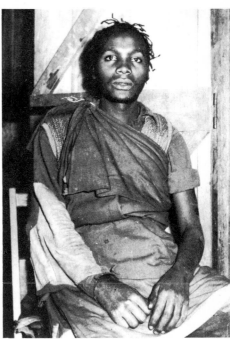

▲ **A Mau Mau terrorist,** "Marshall" Kanji, at the time of his surrender. Mau Mau was a secret society formed by members of the Kikuyu, the largest tribe in the British colony of Kenya. From 1952 they murdered and mutilated white settlers, and also black Africans they considered disloyal. The British government interned thousands of Kikuyus and imprisoned the nationalist leader Jomo Kenyatta as the supposed head of Mau Mau.

◀ **British soldiers search a Greek Orthodox priest** in Cyprus. The majority of Cypriots were Greek, and hoped for enosis (union with Greece). But the minority were Turks, long-standing enemies of the Greeks; and Britain, the colonial authority, was determined to hold on to Cyprus as a military base. In 1955 Greek Cypriots launched a resistance movement E.O.K.A., led by General George Grivas, and years of terrorism and reprisals followed.

Science and Communication

The great advances of the fifties were made in the sciences connected with communications, and above all in electronics.

In 1948 the Bell Telephone Laboratories devised the transistor, a tiny object made of special metals. It was much superior to the radio valve because it could be hundreds of times smaller, used less electrical current and did not overheat. The transistor made it possible to manufacture millions of cheap portable radios; it also helped to make computers cheaper to run and more reliable.

Basically, computers are highly complex calculating machines into which you can feed facts and ideas as well as numbers. All information is stored in "memory banks" which can be tapped by the computer or its user. And once the proper instructions have been fed into it, the computer can perform any logical or mathematical operation at fantastic speeds.

Though they were only coming into wider use in the late fifties, computers promised to revolutionise millions of jobs. A computer can solve problems, act as a records office, work out pay packets and suggest business decisions. And when combined with other machines it can cut out human work altogether. A computer could control traffic or guide an aircraft down to a landing field; it could even run a whole factory.

These were exciting years for other sciences too. The early exploration of space (page 52) brought a wealth of information. It also led to a method of world-wide communication by bouncing radio signals off the Moon and artificial satellites.

Other scientific discoveries included medical breakthroughs such as cortisone for rheumatism and the Salk vaccine for poliomyelitis. Perhaps the most hopeful sign for the future was the peaceful use of nuclear energy (page 32).

▲ **The computer as the enemy of man.** A good many people felt this way. Some thought machines would make men their slaves; others feared they would go haywire and make disastrous mistakes.

▲ **An early computer,** the Ferranti Mark 1 of 1950, like something out of science fiction. Later models were sleeker and more compact.

▲ **Model of a Hovercraft** with its test pilot, inventor (Christopher Cockerell) and designer. It made its first Channel crossing in 1959.

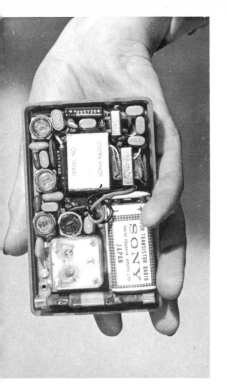

▼ **The introduction of long-playing records** and light, inexpensive record players turned millions of people into record collectors. The LP made it possible to listen to music—or speech—without irritating interruptions.

A radio you could hold in the palm of your hand was one of the revolutions of the fifties. happened because radio valves could be replaced by tiny transistors. Run by batteries, e transistor radio became a handy portable that could be taken anywhere.

Group round a tape recorder rehearsing a ay. During the fifties tape recorders became ss expensive and more accurate, and so more popular. They work by converting sound into electrical pulses. The pulses "record" by creating magnetised patterns on a coating of iron particles spread over the tape. When the tape is played back, the patterns and pulses are reconverted and amplified.

Jets, Rockets and Space

Rockets of incredible power were developed as weapons by the great powers. Russia was the first to send them out into space.

▲ **V2 rockets at Peenemünde,** 1944. Germany's "secret weapon", used on both Paris and London.

▶ **Robert H. Goddard** at work with his team, 1940. Goddard pioneered rocketry in the United States down to his death in 1945. He did valuable work as early as World War One, and in 1926 successfully launched the first liquid-fuel rockets, which rose to a height of a few hundred feet. But even then little attention was paid to Goddard's work, whereas the Russian pioneer K. E. Tsiolkovsky was honoured in his own country. This difference of attitude largely explains Russia's early success in the "space race".

Towards the end of World War Two both Germany and the Allies produced jet fighters. Jet engines are driven by a blast of gas sent through them by burning fuel. By 1945 jets were flying at hundreds of miles per hour.

Rockets are capable of fantastic speeds, and can be guided by remote control. When equipped with explosive "warheads" they are deadly weapons. As early as 1944 Germany had a missile, the V2, which could hit London carrying a powerful T.N.T. warhead.

After the war many German rocket experts went to work in the United States. Both the U.S.A. and Russia developed guided missiles with thermo-nuclear (H-bomb) warheads. These were capable of crossing continents and oceans, and could be guided on to targets on land or in the air.

Serious work on other uses of rockets had been slow to develop in the United States. Then, in October 1957, came Russia's startling announcement that she had launched Sputnik 1. This was a metal ball carried to a height of 18,000 miles by rockets. When th rockets had done their work, Sputnik continued to orbit (circle) the Earth held in place by the force of gravity.

The Sputnik was thus an artificia satellite. (A satellite is a planet or moo that moves round a larger body.) Th first two Sputniks were not placed a quite the right height, and eventuall fell to earth. But most later satellit could well remain in orbit for centurie

American satellites were sent up i 1958. They carried scientific equip ment that sent back much informatior including the discovery of two zones c radiation circling the globe (the Va Allen belts).

Then, in 1959, rockets were fired fa beyond the Earth. Russia's Luna missed the Moon and ended by orbitin the Sun. Luna 2 hit the Moon. An Luna 3 went round it and took th first photographs of the side of th Moon we never see from Earth.

By this time the question had begu to be asked: how long before ma himself sets out into space?

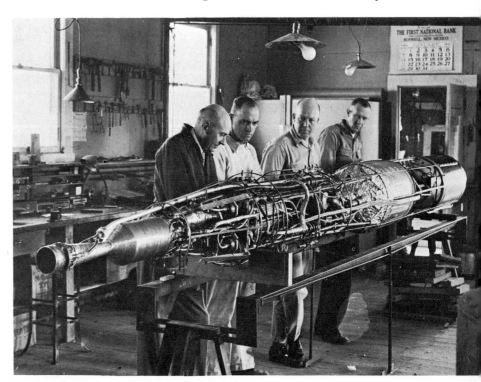

◆ **"Breaking the sound barrier"** was an apt way of describing supersonic flight, for there was a noise like an explosion as an aircraft reached a speed faster than sound. Geoffrey de Havilland broke the sound barrier in 1946 when his plane went into a dive that caused it to break up; de Havilland himself was killed. The first level supersonic flight was made on October 14th 1947 by Captain Charles E. Jaeger (right) in "Glamorous Glennis" (left), a Bell XS-1 rocket plane, over Muroc, California.

Wernher von Braun, the German rocket expert mainly responsible for the V2. He later worked for the U.S. Army, designed the rocket for *Explorer*, and directed U.S. efforts in the "space race".

Sergei Korolev masterminded the Soviet space effort. He was in charge of a rocket research group from the thirties, and designed the Sputniks and later the manned Russian spacecraft of the sixties.

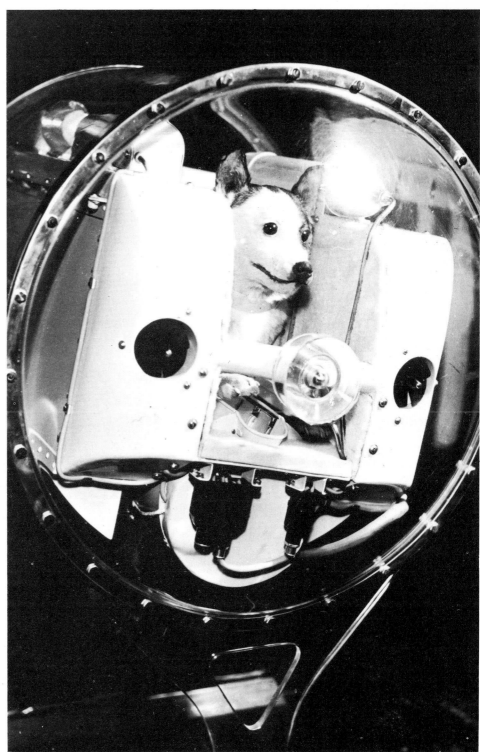

▲ **The first creature in space** was Laika, a mongrel terrier, who was sent up in a capsule with Sputnik 2 in November 1957. Many scientists had believed that no living creature would be able to stand the strain of travel in in space at speeds of 18,000 m.p.h. or more. But if a dog could survive, so could a man—if either could be brought down to Earth.

The Main Events

The most dangerous events of the forties and fifties came out of the Cold War. But the death-throes of the colonial empires, and wars and revolutions among the newly independent nations, added to the complications of world affairs.

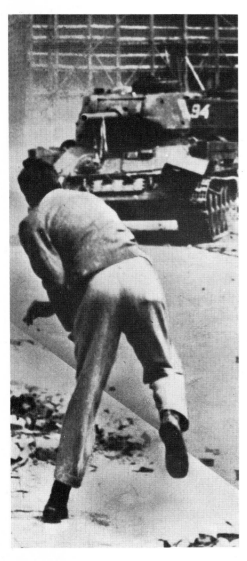

1953: East German rioter in action.

1957: Evil forces menacing a Negro child. From a Soviet cartoon.

1946

January: De Gaulle resigns as French President; end of republican unity. Albania declared a People's Republic.
February: Peron becomes President of Argentina.
March: Churchill makes "Iron Curtain" speech at Fulton, Missouri.
May: Communist successes in Czech elections. Klement Gottwald, Communist leader, becomes Prime Minister.
June: Italy votes to become a republic.
July: Philippines become independent of U.S.A.
September: Greeks vote for monarchy. Bulgaria becomes People's Republic.
October: United Nations General Assembly meets.
General
End of Nuremberg trials of war criminals.
British and French troops leave Syria and Lebanon.
Britain recognises independence of Transjordan.
Russian troops withdraw from Iran (Persia).
Music: operas by Britten, *Rape of Lucretia*, and Prokofiev, *War and Peace*.

1947

February: fuel crisis in Britain.
March: Truman Doctrine, resulting in immediate air for Greek and Turkish governments. Revolt against French in Madagascar.
June: General Marshall proposes further aid for Europe. Anti-trade-union Taft-Hartley Act passed in U.S. over Truman's veto.
August: India and Pakistan independent.
October: Founding of Cominform, Communist information organisation used to exercise Russian control over world's Communist Parties. Benelux, customs union between Belgium, Holland and Luxembourg.
November: Britain—Princess Elizabeth marries Philip, later Duke of Edinburgh.
General
Kon-Tiki expedition.
Book: Albert Camus, *The Plague*. Edinburgh Arts Festival started.

1948

January: Burma independent. Gandhi assassinated by Hindu extremist.
February: Communist takeover in Czechoslovakia.
March: Brussels Treaty. U.S. Congress passes Marshall Aid Act.
April: Communist constitution in Romania. O.E.E.C. set up in Paris.
May: partition of Palestine; Transjordan and Egypt invade. Nationalist Party wins elections in South Africa: policy of separating races (apartheid).
June: Yugoslavia expelled from Cominform.
July: Berlin Blockade starts.
September: Count Bernadotte, U.N. mediator in Palestine, assassinated by Jewish terrorists.
November: Truman unexpectedly re-elected President.
December: Britain—National Service (conscription).
General
Antibiotics, LPs, transistors.
Auguste Piccard's bathyscape for deep-sea exploration.

1949

January: Communist countries grouped economically in C.O.M.E.C.O.N.
February: end of clothes rationing in Britain.
April: N.A.T.O. alliance. Eire breaks last links with Britain.
May: Council of Europe set up at Strasbourg. Berlin Blockade ends. Federal Republic (West Germany) set up.
October: China declared People's Republic. German Democratic Republic (East Germany) set up. End of Greek Civil War.
December: Holland recognises independence of Indonesia.
General
Britain and some other countries devalue currencies. First Russian atomic tests.
Discovery of cortisone and neomycin.
Book: George Orwell, *1984*.
Plays: T. S. Eliot, *The Cocktail Party*; Arthur Miller, *Death of a Salesman*. Film: Carol Reed, *The Third Man*.

1950

January: Alger Hiss, U.S. State Department officer, imprisoned for perjury (concealing membership of Communist Party).
March: Klaus Fuchs, British scientist, imprisoned for passing atomic secrets to Russia.
June: North Korean invasion of South Korea; condemned by U.N. Security Council, who ask members of U.N. to help South Koreans.
September: United Nations landing at Inchon. Britain extends National Service to two years. European Payments Union set up.
October: Chinese take control in Tibet.
November: Chinese enter Korean War.
General
Arab Palestine becomes part of Jordan (previously Transjordan).
Death of Bernard Shaw, aged 94.
Book: C. P. Snow, *The Masters*. Films: Jean Cocteau, *Orphée*; Akira Kurosawa, *Rashomon*. Music: Hindemith, *Harmony of the World* symphony.

1951

March: Czech Communist Party purged.
April: Truman dismisses MacArthur from Far Eastern command. Paris Treaty sets up six-nation coal and steel authority (Schuman Plan). Aneurin Bevan and Harold Wilson resign from British Labour Government over charges for National Health prescriptions. Mussadeq takes power in Iran.
June: British diplomats Burgess and Maclean defect to Russia.
July: King Abdullah of Jordan assassinated.
October: Conservatives come to power in Britain.
November: Peron re-elected in Argentina.
General
Iran: nationalisation of Anglo-Iranian Oil Co. creates crisis.
Festival of Britain.
Electric power produced from atomic energy.
Painting: Salvador Dali, *Christ of St John on the Cross*. Music: Britten, *Billy Budd*; Stravinsky, *Rake's Progress*. Book: Salinger, *Catcher in the Rye*.

▶ **English pop star Tommy Steele** began his career in the fifties.

1952
February: Greece and Turkey join N.A.T.O. Britain: George V dies; succeeded by Elizabeth II. Battista takes power in Cuba.
May: West European powers agree to set up European Defence Community (E.D.C.).
July: General Neguib takes power in Egypt; King Farouk abdicates. In Argentina, Eva Peron dies.
October: British A-bomb test. State of Emergency in Kenya; arrest of Kenya African Union leaders.
November: U.S.A.: first H-bomb test in Pacific; Eisenhower elected president. Czechoslovakia: former Communist leader Slansky and others hanged.
General
Use of radio isotopes in medicine.
Michael Ventris deciphers "Linear B", ancient Cretan script.
Films: Orson Welles, *Othello*; Vittorio de Sica, *Umberto D.* Cinerama introduced. Books: Hemingway, *The Old Man and the Sea*; Angus Wilson, *Hemlock and After.*

1953
March: death of Stalin; Georgi Malenkov Chairman of U.S.S.R. Council of Ministers.
April: Jomo Kenyatta convicted of managing Mau Mau.
May: Everest climbed.
June: Rising in East Berlin. Rosenbergs executed in U.S.A. Coronation of Elizabeth II.
July: Korean armistice signed at Panmunjon.
August: Iran: fall of Mussadeq. Russia explodes H-bomb.
September: Khrushchev First Secretary of Central Committee of Soviet Communist Party.
October: British army intervenes in British Guiana to stop supposed Communist takeover. Federation of North and South Rhodesia and Nyasaland.
General
Colour TV in U.S.A.
Sculpture: Reg Butler, *Unknown Political Prisoner.*
Films: Fellini, *I Vitelloni*; *The Robe* (CinemaScope).
Books: John Wain, *Hurry on Down*; Ian Fleming, *Casino Royale* (first James Bond story).

1954
March: siege of Dien Bien Phu, which falls in May. H-bomb tests at Bikini by U.S.A.
April: Colonel Nasser Prime Minister of Egypt; replaces Neguib as President in November.
July: armistice in Indo-China, followed by independence of Communist North Vietnam and South Vietnam, Laos and Cambodia.
August: French Assembly rejects E.D.C. agreement. Iranian oil problem solved.
September: S.E.A.T.O. alliance to defend South-East Asia from Communism.
October: Paris agreements end occupation of Germany; West Germany joins N.A.T.O.; Western European Union set up. Trieste divided between Yugoslavia and Italy. British agree to evacuate Suez Canal Zone.
November: beginning of rebellion in Algeria.
December: U.S. Senate censures Senator McCarthy.
General
Books: Kingsley Amis, *Lucky Jim*; Tolkien, *Lord of the Rings*. Film: Fellini, *La Strada.*

1955
February: Malenkov resigns. Bulganin and Khrushchev ("B and K") become Russian leaders.
April: Churchill resigns, Eden becomes British Prime Minister. Bandung conference of Afro-Asian countries.
May: Communist states form military alliance, the Warsaw Pact. Occupation of Austria ends. Khrushchev and Bulganin visit Yugoslavia.
September: Peron overthrown in Argentina.
October: Bao Dai, Emperor of Vietnam, deposed; republic proclaimed.
November: South Africa withdraws from United Nations after criticisms of her racial policies.
General
Baghdad Pact links Britain, Irak, Turkey, Iran.
Enosis crisis in Cyprus.
Commercial television in Britain.
Salk vaccine for poliomyelitis.
Book: Nabokov, *Lolita*. Play: Beckett, *Waiting for Godot*. Music: Tippett, *Midsummer Marriage.*

1956
January: the Sudan becomes independent.
February: 20th Communist Party Congress, Moscow: Khrushchev's speech denouncing Stalin.
March: Archbishop Makarios, Cypriot leader, deported to Seychelles islands. Tunisia and Morocco independent.
April: Cominform dissolved. Khrushchev and Bulganin visit Britain.
June: last British troops leave Suez Canal Zone. Riots in Poznan, Poland.
July: Nasser nationalises Suez Canal.
October: Gomulka, national-minded Communist, takes power in Poland. New government in Hungary, including non-Communists ("Hungarian Revolution"). Israel attacks Egypt.
November: Russians suppress Hungarian Revolution. Anglo-French expedition: Suez fiasco. Eisenhower re-elected as U.S. President.
General: Aldermaston march. Calder Hall opened.
Book: Colin Wilson, *The Outsider*; play: John Osborne, *Look Back in Anger.*

1957
January: Harold Macmillan becomes British Prime Minister. The Saar reunited with (West) Germany.
March: Ghana becomes independent. Treaty of Rome setting up Common Market. European Atomic Community (Euratom) established.
May: first British hydrogen bomb.
August: Malayan Federation independent.
General
Sputniks 1 and 2.
U.S.A. in economic difficulties.
Desegregation crisis in U.S.A.: Federal troops sent to Little Rock.
Beginning of International Geophysical Year, with programme of international research in earth sciences.
Fidel Castro begins rebellion in Cuba.
Books: Jack Kerouac, *On the Road*; John Braine, *Room at the Top*; Patrick White, *Voss*. Film: Lean, *Bridge on the River Kwai*. Music: Bernstein and Robbins, *West Side Story.*

1958
January: Formation of West Indies Federation.
February: Egypt and Syria form United Arab Republic (U.A.R.). Kingdoms of Iraq and Jordan form Arab Federation. Full economic union of Benelux.
March: Khrushchev dominances leadership in U.S.S.R. Yemen joins U.A.R.
April: French army in a state of revolt in Algeria.
May: De Gaulle takes power in France.
June: execution of Nagy, Hungarian Prime Minister during 1956 revolution.
July: revolution in Iraq: King Feisal killed. U.S. troops in Lebanon and British troops in Jordan to protect their independence. Britain: race riots in Notting Hill, London; introduction of life peerages.
October: Russian loan arranged for Egypt's Aswan Dam. Ayub Khan sets up military government in Pakistan. New Pope, John XXXIII.
General: books: Pasternak, *Dr Zhivago*; Durrell, *Justine*. Film: Wajda, *Ashes and Diamonds*. Music: Searle, *Diary of a Madman.*

1959
January: Castro takes power in Cuba. New African state, Mali, formed from Senegal and French Sudan.
February: Agreement on Cyprus problem between Britain, Greece and Turkey. Macmillan and Selwyn Lloyd (Foreign Secretary) visit U.S.S.R.
March: Makarios returns to Cyprus from exile. Revolt against Chinese in Tibet; Tibetan religious leader, Dalai Lama, flees to India. Iraq withdraws from Baghdad Pact. Mao gives up chairmanship of Chinese Republic.
June: Singapore becomes self-governing.
October: Conservatives re-elected in Britain under Macmillan. Luna 3 takes photos of hidden side of Moon.
November: European Free Trade Association (E.F.T.A.) formed by Britain and six other European countries ("the seven") as alternative to Common Market. Border clashes between India and China.
General: opening of Guggenheim Art Museum, New York. Designer: Frank Lloyd Wright. Play: Behan, *The Hostage.*

Who Was Who

Adenauer, Konrad (1876-1967). Anti-Nazi Mayor of Cologne in Germany, twice imprisoned under Hitler. After the war he became leader of the newly formed Christian Democratic Party, which won West Germany's first free election in 1949.

Adenauer became Chancellor of Germany and stayed in power until his retirement in 1963. He followed a strong anti-Communist policy, refused to recognise the separate existence of East Germany, and in later years worked closely with De Gaulle.

Attlee, Clement (1883-1967). British Prime Minister in the Labour Government of 1945-51. A social worker in London's East End, Mayor of Stepney, and an M.P. from 1922; leader of the Labour Party from 1935.

Attlee was Churchill's deputy during the war. As Prime Minister after it he presided over the setting up of the Welfare State and Indian independence. But he was not so much a policy maker as an effective leader, skilful at keeping together a Cabinet team of conflicting personalities.

Ben-Gurion, David (1886-1973). Israeli leader, born in Poland. In 1906 he emigrated to Palestine and became a farmer. He served with the British against the Turks, and from the time of the Mandate he aimed at an independent Jewish state rather than the vague "national home" promised by the Balfour Declaration. Ben-Gurion founded the Jewish trade union organisation, Histadrut, and became leader of the Labour Party, Mapai. When Britain's pro-Jewish policy changed in 1939, he encouraged Jewish resistance. Ben-Gurion was Israel's first Prime Minister (1948-53), and held office again 1955-1963.

Bevan, Aneurin ("Nye") (1897-1960). Welsh politician, a miner's son who became leader of the Labour Party's left wing (i.e. those who wanted more radical policies). He was M.P. for Ebbw Vale from 1929 and, as Minister of Health in the 1945-50 government, set up the National Health Service.

In 1951 Bevan became Minister of Labour, but he and Harold Wilson resigned from the government because they objected to the expense of rearmament and the charges introduced for Health Service prescriptions. In the fifties Bevan failed to gain control of the Labour Party, though he and his followers—the "Bevanites"—were a force in British politics. Bevan bitterly opposed Gaitskell's right-wing policies, though at the time of his death Bevan had dropped his opposition to Britain having her own H-bombs.

Bevin, Ernest (1881-1951). British trade unionist and politician. Although poorly educated, "Ernie" Bevin made the Transport and General Workers' Union the biggest and most powerful union in Britain. But as wartime Minister of Labour and National Service he limited the power of the unions in the national interest. As Foreign Secretary from 1945 he quickly became hostile to Stalin and committed to the alliance with the U.S.A. His policy over Palestine was a disastrous failure.

Churchill, Winston Spencer (1874-1965). Britain's inspiring leader in World War Two, nevertheless voted out of office in 1945. He spent much of his time writing his account of *The Second World War*. Prime Minister again (1951-55), he encouraged closer European co-operation but valued the Commonwealth and the American alliance too much to commit Britain to Europe. After retiring in 1955, he began his *History of the English-Speaking Peoples*.

Dulles, John Foster (1888-1959). U.S. Secretary of State, in charge of foreign policy from 1952 to 1959. Dulles followed a policy of firm anti-Communism. He was sometimes condemned for "brinkmanship"— his proclaimed policy of being ready to go to the very brink of world war. His brother, Allan Dulles, was head of the C.I.A., the American Intelligence Agency.

Aneurin Bevan: Welsh champion of the working man.

Eden, Anthony (1897-   ). British politician, Foreign Secretary under Churchill from 1940, and regarded as his natural successor. Foreign Secretary again (1951-55), he became Prime Minister on Churchill's retirement.

Eden's career was blighted almost at once by the Suez crisis. He thought of Nasser as another Hitler who had to be stopped in his tracks before he grew too strong. But the objectives of the Suez expedition were poorly thought out, and world reaction was underestimated. When Eden ordered a cease-fire (much to French disgust) it was the first sign that Britain's attempts to maintain a world-wide influence were beyond her strength. Eden resigned within months of Suez, giving ill health as the reason.

Eisenhower, Dwight D. (1890-1969). American soldier, commander of U.S. troops in Europe from 1942; he was in charge of the North African, Italian and Normandy landings.

After a period of semi-retirement he was called to be Supreme Commander of N.A.T.O. in 1951. In 1952 a popular campaign ("I Like Ike") persuaded him to run as Republican Party candidate for President. He was elected, and although not a particularly dynamic President, kept tremendous personal popularity—so much so that he was re-elected in 1956, although his party did badly.

Gaitskell, Hugh (1903-63). British Labour Party leader, succeeding Attlee in 1955. A university lecturer and civil servant, Gaitskell had been Minister of Fuel and Power (1947-50) and Chancellor of the Exchequer (1951).

As leader he tried to remove nationalisation from Labour's programme, and in general to make the party less doctrinaire. This deeply divided Labour supporters and led to bitter quarrels with Bevan and his followers.

Gandhi, Mahatma (1869-1948). Indian religious and political leader, a London-trained barrister who became active in fighting for Indian rights in South Africa. Later, as a holy man—but a shrewd politician too—he led non-violent resistance to British rule in India. A few months after the independence he had done so much to achieve, Gandhi was shot dead by a Hindu who blamed him for the partition of India.

de Gaulle, Charles (1890-1970). French soldier and political leader. He fought in World War One and later foresaw the importance of tanks and other mobile elements in future wars; but his views had little influence. When France fell to the (mobile) German attack in 1940, De Gaulle set up a Free French government in London which served as a rallying point for resistance to the Germans.

De Gaulle became France's first post-war President but soon resigned. His proud, obstinate, independent character made him unsuited to the compromises of party politics. He made it clear that he was ready to return to politics if offered wider authority.

As the years passed, this seemed less and less likely. But the weakness of French governments and the Algerian revolt led to a political crisis. De Gaulle was called, framed a new constitution giving the French President wide powers, and was himself elected President.

Powerful support for De Gaulle came from the French army in Algeria, which believed a military man would never grant independence. By 1959 it was becoming obvious that it had misunderstood De Gaulle's character.

Gomulka, Wladislaw (1905-   ). Polish Communist leader, an oil worker who later studied in Moscow and operated in the Polish underground during the war. He held the powerful position of First Secretary of the Communist Party in post-war Poland, but in 1948 he was expelled and even imprisoned for a time. His return to power in 1956, after hard bargaining with Khrushchev, meant a slightly freer atmosphere and less Russian-controlled policies.

King, Martin Luther (1929-68). American negro leader. He was a Baptist minister at Montgomery, Alabama, where he led a boycott of the segregated bus service (1954). In the fifties King and his Southern Christian Conference took the lead in marching and demonstrating for civil rights; their non-violent tactics won wide support from both negroes and whites.

Nikita Khrushchev: Russian bear in the Cold War.

Soldier turned politician: **de Gaulle.**

Khrushchev, Nikita Sergeyevich (1894-1971). Russian leader. He joined the Communist Party in 1918 and held many important positions in the thirties. After Stalin's death he took over the key post of First Secretary of the Communist Party, and after Malenkov's resignation in 1955 was clearly the most important Russian leader.

Khrushchev denounced Stalin's tyranny in 1956, released many political prisoners, and allowed more (though still limited) freedom of thought and discussion. He also put forward the idea that war with the West might not be inevitable (as Communists had believed), but that peaceful competition might win over the West to Communism. "Peaceful co-existence" became a theme of Russian propaganda.

Whereas Stalin disliked speaking in public and never left Russia after he took power, Khrushchev was a wordy, exuberant man, fond of quoting Russian proverbs, who visited the U.S.A., Britain, India, and other countries.

Macmillan, Harold (1894-   ). British politician who rose to prominence as Conservative Minister of Housing (1951), successfully building 300,000 houses a year. Later Foreign Secretary and Chancellor of the Exchequer under Eden, he was an enthusiastic supporter of the Suez adventure.

But when Eden resigned in January 1957, he was succeeded by Macmillan, who managed to mend Anglo-American relations and visited Khrushchev in Moscow. And as Britain was becoming affluent in the late fifties, Macmillan became very popular and was nicknamed "Supermac". He won the 1959 election with no difficulty.

Makarios, Archbishop (1913-   ). Archbishop of Cyprus (Greek Orthodox Church) since 1950. As leader of the island's Greek community he worked for *enosis* (union with Greece). The British government suspected that he was linked with the terrorist E.O.K.A. movement and in 1956 deported him to the Seychelles islands in the Indian Ocean. A year later he was allowed to go to Greece, but not to return to Cyprus.

By 1959 Makarios had changed his mind. He accepted that enosis could not be carried out, and took office as the first President of a separate, independent Republic of Cyprus. (Britain was satisfied by being granted sovereign rights over military bases.) Makarios then worked to restore friendly relations between Greek and Turkish Cypriot Cypriots.

Mao Tse-tung (1893-   ). Chinese Communist leader. He fought with the republican army that overthrew the Chinese emperor, studied at Peking University, and became a Communist.

In the twenties Mao spent his time organising propaganda among the peasants. Most Communist leaders believed that the revolution would be made by town workers, but Chiang Kai-shek struck at them ruthlessly. Mao emerged as leader of virtually a new Communist Party, based on peasant support.

After the defeat of Japan and Chiang's Nationalists Mao was Chairman of the Chinese People's Republic (1949-59), retiring after the failure of the "Great Leap Forward"; but as Secretary of the Communist Party he remained potentially powerful.

Mussadeq (1880-1967). Iranian Prime Minister, 1951-53. He nationalised the huge Anglo-Iranian Oil Company and attempted to operate it with Iranian workers—without much success.

Mussadeq was a highly theatrical personality, often making speeches from his bed and weeping copiously. He failed to sell Iranian oil abroad and was overthrown by the Shah, probably with U.S. help. A new oil agreement followed between Iran and an international group of companies. Mussadeq was imprisoned for three years.

Nagy, Imre (1896-1958). Hungarian Communist. He was taken prisoner by the Russians in World War One, was converted to Communism, and fought on the side of the Russian Red Army.

Nagy spent fifteen years in Russia (1929-44) while Hungary was under semi-fascist rule, and became a minister in post-war Communist governments. He was dropped in 1949 because of his independent outlook, and again after a period as Prime Minister (1953-55).

During the 1956 uprising Nagy became leader of a non-Communist government which was suppressed by the Russians. He took refuge in the Yugoslav Embassy, was tricked into coming out, deported to Roumania, and later put on trial and executed.

Nasser, Colonel Gamal Abdul (1915-70). Egyptian soldier who took a leading part in the overthrow of King Farouk in 1952. He gradually took over from the first leader of the revolution, General Neguib, becoming Prime Minister in 1954; President in 1956.

Soldier turned politician: **Nasser.**

Under Nasser, Egypt became a one-party, vaguely socialist state. Nasser's firm anti-colonialism made him admired by many in the Arab world, and weakened the influence of pro-Western monarchies such as Jordan and Iraq.

Nehru, Jawaharlal (1889-1964). India's first Prime Minister (1947-64). His policy was one of "non-alignment"—of not taking sides in the Cold War. His attempts to form a non-aligned bloc were only partly successful, though the Afro-Asian conference at Bandung (1955) and the Indian-Egyptian-Yugoslav meeting (1956) seemed promising.

Spaak, Paul-Henri (1889-1972). Belgian politician. A socialist, many times Foreign Minister of Belgium, Prime Minister (1938-39, 1947-50) and Deputy Prime Minister (1961-65). He was a supporter of the Atlantic alliance (N.A.T.O. Secretary-General, 1957-61), but was best known as "Mr Europe", presiding over the European Coal and Steel Community and playing a vital part in negotiating the Treaty of Rome that set up the Common Market.

Stalin, Joseph (1879-1953). Dictator who made Russia a great power, but at terrible cost in human suffering. In his last years Stalin kept his grip on every aspect of Soviet life, including even scientific research and art. Though few even considered opposing him, there were still arrests and executions. Eastern Europe was virtually a Russian colony in which faithful Stalinists copied the dictator's purges.

Sukarno (1901-70). Indonesian nationalist leader, imprisoned by the Dutch in the twenties and exiled in the thirties. He co-operated with the Japanese invaders of the Indies and was strong enough to declare Indonesia a republic at the end of the war. Though Sukarno and his government were at one time captured by Dutch troops, independence was achieved with the help of U.N. pressure.

Sukarno was a great orator with a huge popular following. He changed Indonesia into a "Guided Democracy" (with himself as guide!) and managed to hold together his poor, badly divided country. But he failed to solve its economic problems, and his "anti-imperialist" line became more anti-American.

Tito, Marshal (1892-   ). Yugoslav Communist leader, often jailed for his political activities in the thirties. He went underground, becoming known as "Tito" instead of Josip Broz, his real name. He also spent some time in Russia.

Tito became leader of the Yugoslav Communist Party in 1940, just before the German invasion. He emerged as chief of the partisans (resistance fighters). Thanks to the mountainous landscape, the partisans were effective guerrillas and eventually liberated most of their country.

Tito then took power as a popular Communist President, not a Russian stooge. And when he broke with Stalin the Yugoslav people supported him. He developed his own, more liberal brand of Communism, refused to take sides in the Cold War, and tried to strengthen his ties with the other "non-aligned" states such as Egypt and India.

Truman, Harry S. (1884-1972). U.S. President, 1945-52. Truman was not a well known figure in politics in 1944, when he was chosen as Vice-President (an important, but not a very influential office in the U.S.A.). President Roosevelt's death unexpectedly promoted Truman to President; and (equally unexpectedly) he proved a great one.

His first really big decision was that A-bombs should be dropped on Hiroshima and Nagasaki to shorten the war. Perhaps no other President has had to make so many great decisions: Marshall Aid, the Berlin Airlift, the setting up of N.A.T.O., intervention in Korea. The Truman Doctrine ensured that America would not return to her pre-war isolationism.

Skiffle Band

During the 1950s, popular music went through a dramatic change with the advent of skiffle and rock bands. This project shows how you can form your own band using easy-to-make instruments.

Materials

Washboard
30 wooden dowels, 1 cm in dia × 20 cm long
wooden frame

Drums
5 litre paint tin
garden wire
inner tube
dowels

Maracas
balloons
string
wallpaper adhesive or flour and water mixture
newspaper
50 gm split peas
dowels, 1 cm dia × 20 cm long

Box bass
tea chest or similar box, 50 cm square
drill
length of cord
broom handle or 2 cm dia dowel
nail

The Origins of Skiffle

Towards the end of the last century, a completely new kind of music called "jazz" came into being in the city of New Orleans, U.S.A. It was first heard in the Negro areas of the city, and came from the natural desire of the Negro people to express their feelings in song and rhythm. Within twenty years, the popularity of jazz had spread all over the world. In many cases, people could not afford to buy expensive instruments such as trumpets, basses and drums, but their desire to make music overcame their poverty and they made their own instruments from whatever they could find.

The early bands which used home-made instruments to play jazz were called Spasm bands. They made guitars and banjos from old cigar boxes and cheese boxes, trumpets from metal funnels, basses from packing cases and used all manner of things for percussion instruments. In many cases the music which they made was as good as that of bands which used 'proper' instruments. These Spasm bands often played at parties which were known in the Mississippi as Skiffles, and gradually skiffle became the name used to describe this type of music.

The first record of skiffle music was made in America in 1948 by "Dan Burley's Skiffle Boys" and a year later the first English skiffle group was formed by the "Crane River Jazz Band". It was not really until 1954 that skiffle became well known in England through such groups as Ken Colyer and Lonnie Donegan, whose music inspired many young people to form their own skiffle groups.

Most of the professional groups in England used proper guitars and banjos, together with a double bass. The only home-made instrument used was the wash-board, but this rather defeated the original object of skiffle as "home made" music. There were, however, many young groups who followed the original idea of skiffle and made excellent music with the aid of home-made instruments and good voices.

The following instruments are all designed to be made very cheaply so that you can make music with your friends without spending a lot of money. If you are lucky enough to own an instrument already, use it to fit in with other home-made instruments. The more "home-made" your sound is, the better.

Percussion Instruments

Percussion instruments include anything which is struck to produce a sound, such as a drum. Generally, these are used to set a rhythm around which the melody is played, but in some cases tunes may be played by the percussion section of the band. Most skiffle groups include a metal or wooden washboard, which is played by fitting metal sewing thimbles onto the fingers of both hands and lightly running these over the serrations on the washboard to produce a rhythmic clicking sound.

Washboard

If you find it difficult to obtain a washboard, you can make one using about 30 wooden dowels or bamboo sticks approx. 1 cm. diameter by 20 cm. long, nailed to a wooden frame (fig. 1). Drill holes for the nails to avoid splitting the dowels and make sure that the heads are sunk well into the surface of the wood to avoid accidents.

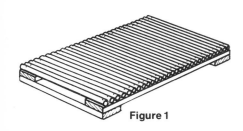

Figure 1

Drums

Drums can be made out of a 5 litre paint tin which should be cleaned out to increase resonance. Stretch a piece of motor car inner tube or other sheet rubber as tightly as possible over the open end of the tin and fix in position by binding garden wire over the rubber just underneath the lip of the tin (fig. 2). You will need to get someone to hold the rubber stretched in place while you wire it on. Twist the ends of the wire together, cut off the surplus rubber and cover the wire with adhesive tape. Study a picture of a military drum and see if you can think of a way of modifying your drum so that the sound can be varied by stretching the rubber more tightly. Play the drum with drumsticks made from pieces of wooden dowel with the ends rounded off. Try using different sized tins to produce different notes.

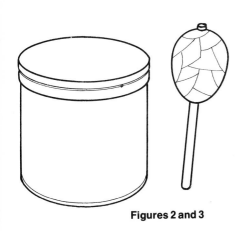

Figures 2 and 3

Maracas

Although not normally associated with skiffle, maracas add a pleasant sound to the rhythm section of many types of music. Inflate two small balloons to about 8 cm. diameter and tie the ends with string. Prepare about $\frac{1}{4}$ litre of wallpaper adhesive (or flour and water paste), tear up some old newspapers into small squares and paste these onto the balloons evenly until you have built up about six or eight layers all round the balloons, with the exception of the neck which should be left sticking out. Leave to dry overnight, then undo the string and remove the balloons. Make a hole 1 cm. diameter opposite the hole where the neck was and put about 50 grammes

of split peas inside each. Glue a piece of 1 cm. diameter dowel 20 cm. long into each maraca (fig. 3) and paint the outsides. Hold one handle in each hand and shake to produce a rhythm. Listen to Latin American music to hear the types of rhythm played on maracas.

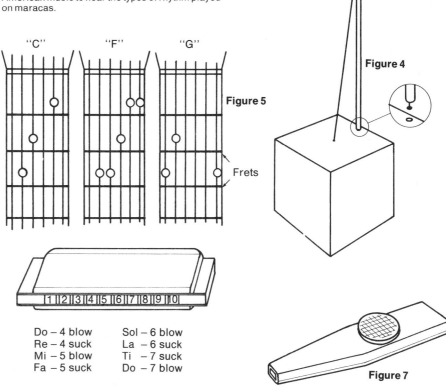

"C"   "F"   "G"

Figure 5

Frets

| 1 | 2 | 3 | 4 | 5 | 6 | 7 | 8 | 9 | 10 |

Do – 4 blow	Sol – 6 blow
Re – 4 suck	La – 6 suck
Mi – 5 blow	Ti – 7 suck
Fa – 5 suck	Do – 7 blow

Figure 6

Figure 4

Figure 7

Stringed Instruments

Box Bass

The box bass is probably the simplest of all stringed instruments to make. You will need a tea chest about 50 cm. square or a similar box made of thin wood. All stringed instruments are made of wood because it is mainly the vibration of the string against the wood which produces the sound.

Drill a hole about 3 mm. diameter in the middle of the bottom and thread a piece of thin cord through the hole, tying a large knot in the end of the string or tying it to a nail to stop it pulling through the hole. Cut a notch in one end of a broom handle or 2 cm. diameter dowel 1 m. long and drive a nail into the other end with the head of the nail protruding about 2 cm. Drill a hole large enough to accept the nail head in the position shown and attach the loose end of the cord to the notch in the handle (fig. 4).

To play the bass, stand with one foot on the box and hold the handle with one hand while plucking the cord with the other. As you tighten the cord by moving the handle backwards, the note produced will rise. The bass can be made to sound better by making two holes in the front which will allow the sound to come out.

Banjos and Guitars

Other stringed instruments such as guitars and banjos are not easy to make if they are to sound effective. If you look around, you should be able to find a guitar for around £5—it would probably cost as much as this to make one. An important point to look for when buying a guitar is the closeness of the strings to the frets.

If this distance is too great, you will have difficulty in pressing the strings down onto the finger-board. It is probably easier if you start off with nylon strings, as these are "softer" to handle.

Buy an instruction book when you buy a guitar so that you can learn to play the chords properly. It does not take long to master the playing and changing of three chords, the basis of skiffle and blues music. The best chords to learn first are C, F, and G. (See fig. 5.)

Wind Instruments

Mouth organ or Harmonica

The mouth organ or harmonica is a very useful instrument. It is relatively inexpensive to buy, easy to carry and fairly easy to play. Many singers play a melody on the mouth organ between verses, or some even attach one to a harness around their necks so that they can play another instrument with their hands at the same time.

The best sort of mouth organ to buy is the single row, ten hole type, which is tuned to one key only. If the guitarist is playing the chords C, F and G previously mentioned, a mouth organ in the key of C will be in tune. If he is playing another sequence such as E, A, D, then the mouth organ should be in the key of E. This is known as the base chord. The mouth organ is played with the low notes to your left. Practice playing the tonic sol-fa scale before you begin to learn tunes (fig. 6).

Always keep your mouth organ in its case when you are not using it, as dust and grit will ruin the reeds which vibrate to make the sound.

Kazoo

The kazoo is indispensible to a "do it yourself" band. This usually takes the place of brass instruments and can be very effective with practice. Plastic or metal kazoos are usually fairly easy to buy for a few pence. If you put one end into your mouth and say "der-der", you will hear and feel the tissue vibrating to the sound waves of your voice. Try to find different ways of modulating your voice in order to establish the best method of producing music. Listen to the brass sections of different bands and try to copy the tunes.

A great deal of satisfaction can be had from making music on instruments which you have constructed yourself and there are many more instruments which you can try your hand at making. It is probable that many of the "pop" stars today began their musical careers in the same way. Listen to music played on the radio and try to see how each instrument fits in with the other instruments.

Understanding the Computer

Materials

Abacus (digital computer)

plywood, 6 mm thick
glasspaper
drill
length of wire
jar, 4 or 5 cm in diameter
beads (wooden or plastic)
adhesive glue

Card system (informational computer)

postcards, 14 cm × 9 cm
box, similar size
paper punch
ruler
drill
glasspaper
adhesive glue
panel pins
pen or pencil
scissors
adhesive glue

Introduction

For thousands of years, man has been trying to find faster and more efficient ways of counting numbers to help him in his everyday life. As his needs have become more complex, the computers which he has devised to cope with them have become more complex. Although the word "computer" usually makes one think of an electronic "brain", the word can actually be used to describe any kind of machine which is used to work out something involving numbers.

Computers cannot "think", but can calculate sums at superhuman speeds and store enormous amounts of information in tiny "memory cells". The following project enables you to devise your own simple digital computer or "memory bank".

The Abacus

One of the earliest computers devised by man was the abacus. Although invented a long, long time ago by the Chinese, is still used today in many countries for simple calculations. One normally associates the abacus with teaching young children to count but it is by no means a toy and can be a surprisingly useful piece of equipment to have. It may be made in several different ways, but the method shown is probably as efficient as any.

Cut the parts as shown in fig. 1 from 6 mm. thick plywood, ensuring that the edges are straight. Use glasspaper to smooth the wood making sure that the edges are not sharp. Drill the holes the same diameter as that of your wire and assemble the wooden parts using panel pins and glue as shown in fig. 2.

Cut five wires approx. 40 cm. long and carefully bend them around a small jar about 4 or 5 cm. in diameter, to obtain a smooth curve. Mark off and cut the wires to the correct length to go through the holes (fig. 3).

Thread ten beads onto each wire and put a little glue on each end of the wires before fitting them into the holes in the box. It is important for the beads to pass easily round the curves and it may be necessary to open up the holes in them slightly with a small drill.

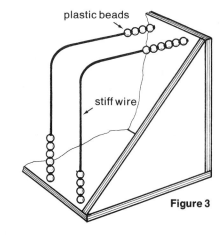

Figure 3

Counting money will be easier if the 2 rows of beads to the right (pence), are of a different colour to the other 3 rows (pounds). You may wish to work out your own colour scheme to suit a certain application.

To use your abacus, begin by pushing up all the beads so that they lie along the top of the wires (in store). The right hand wire indicates units, the next tens, the middle hundreds, and so on. If, for instance, you want to add 359 and 1022, first push down the beads as shown for 359, then push down the appropriate beads for 1022. When one wire is full push up all ten beads and pull down one on the next column to indicate 10 (i.e. carry 1). See fig. 4.

When subtracting, begin by pulling down the first number then lifting up the number which you wish to subtract from it.

You will soon learn to add or subtract lists of figures much more quickly than by working them out on paper. Try to work out how you can multiply and divide on the abacus by moving groups of beads together.

The abacus uses the base 10 for calculations (when 10 is reached in one column, it is carried over to the next column), in the same way as we use it for all written sums, but modern computers often use the base of 2. This is called the binary system and each column can only count up to 1. Thus the first column indicates 1, the second indicates 2, the third 4, then 8, 16, 32, 64 etc.

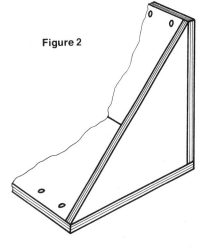

Figure 2

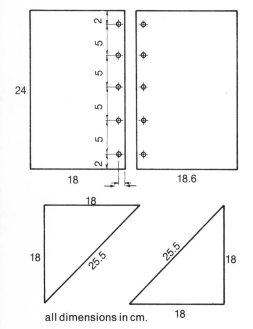

all dimensions in cm.

Figure 1

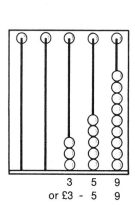

3   5   9
or £3 - 5   9

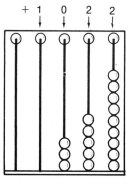

+ 1   0   2   2

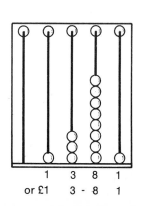

=   1   3   8   1
or £1   3 - 8   1

Figure 4

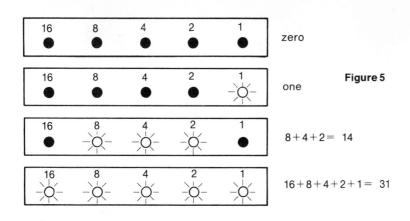

Figure 5

zero

one

$8+4+2= 14$

$16+8+4+2+1= 31$

To use the punch cards simply stack them in the box and, using the master card for reference, insert a knitting needle through one of the characteristic holes you wish to select. Shake the box slightly to release unwanted cards and then lift out the remaining cards with the knitting needle. All the cards which have that characteristic will come out. Remove the cards in the box and replace with those on the knitting needle. Repeat for all the other characteristics you require and then turn the cards over, including the master card, and repeat for the bottom row. The card or cards with the information you require will remain on the knitting needle when you have finished selecting the last characteristic.

Providing that you keep your cards in sets, together with a master card for each particular set, you can use the system for any number of different subjects. Think of different uses to which you can put the system, both for hobbies and for school work. You may wish to collect cookery recipes, for instance, using each hole for a different ingredient.

The Binary Computer

Figure 5 shows the layout of a 5-stage binary indicator, firstly in its zero position and then showing how different numbers are indicated. It is therefore possible for a 5-stage binary counter to count up to 31 $(16+8+4+2+1)$ (or $2^5 - 1$).

Obviously, this system is not as efficient as a written method, but it is ideal for the computer because each section is always in use and thus reduces the necessary number of parts. Comparing our abacus with a binary counter we need 50 beads (or stages) to count up to 100,000, whereas the binary counter only needs 17 stages to count up to the same number.

Unfortunately, a worthwhile electronic binary machine which will transfer figures automatically to the correct section is too complicated and costly to build (approximately £1 for each stage) to be detailed in this book. Your local library should be able to help if you want to find out more about the system.

Digital computers operate on the binary system. They work at great speeds and are used for processing information as well as for making numerical calculations. Analogue computers, which solve specific problems concerned with physical quantities, though less efficient, are equally useful to modern science. Look up both types in your local library to compare the manner in which they work and the kind of problems they can solve.

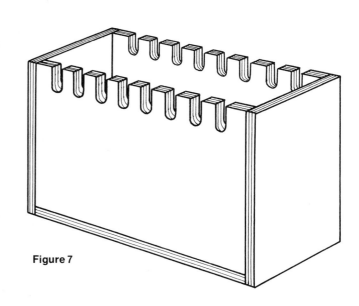

Figure 7

Processing Information

Computers which are used to process *data* or information need an input system, a central processing unit which contains the "memory", and an output. The computer is asked the question by feeding into it a card (called a punch card), which has the coded question punched out in tiny holes. The computer then tries to find information which will correspond with the hole positions in the card. Although these computers, which work electronically, are very complex, you can make a simple mechanical punch card storage system in order to find information quickly which uses the same basic idea as the computer.

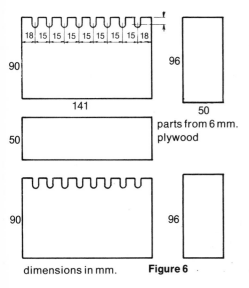

18 15 15 15 15 15 15 15 18

90

141

50

50

90

96

96

50

parts from 6 mm. plywood

dimensions in mm.   **Figure 6**

A Home-Made Data System

The box is designed to suit standard postcards measuring 14 cm. by 9 cm. If the cards which you are using are a different size to this, the front and back of the box should be made not more than 1 mm. larger than your card. Begin by punching holes along the edge of one postcard with a paper punch, then measure the distance from the edge of the card to the centre of the hole (probably about 12 mm. depending on the punch used). This distance will be dimension 'X', so you can now mark out the wooden parts as shown in fig. 6, and drill the 6 mm. holes for the slots. These should then be carefully cut out with a fine-tooth saw. Smooth the faces and edges of the wooden parts with glasspaper and assemble the box with glue and panel pins as shown in fig. 7.

Prepare as many postcards as you wish to use by punching holes to correspond with the slots in the box along the top and bottom of the cards. Do not cut slots in the cards yet.

First decide on the subject area in which you are interested and then work out the different characteristics which you want to select. For instance, if you are interested in motor cars, characteristics which you could include might be body type, engine capacity, engine position, speed, petrol consumption, etc. The box is designed to give up to 16 different characteristics (8 at the top and 8 at the bottom of each card).

A master card is first made as shown in fig 8, giving the particulars of each characteristic required; then information, pictures, etc. are filled in on the postcards (one card for each car). Where a particular characteristic does not apply to a car, the hole in that position is cut out to make a slot (fig. 9). If you cut about $\frac{1}{2}$ cm. from the top left hand corner of each card you will be able to see easily if they are all the correct way up.

Conclusion

It is hoped that this project will help you appreciate man's constant search for better means to achieve the objectives which he sets himself. Computers are not an end product, they are merely machines which are designed to relieve man of the burden of working out things the 'long winded' way. A computer cannot do anything which a man cannot do, because it can only re-organise things which man has 'programmed' it to do, but it can do many things much faster.

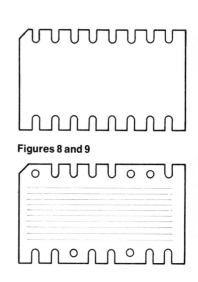

Figures 8 and 9

Index

Note: numbers in bold refer to illustrations

"Abstract Expressionism", 46
Accidents, on road, 45
Adenauer, Konrad, 56
Advertising, 42, **43**
"Affluent society", 42
Africa, 3
"Age of Affluence", 3
Agriculture, Soviet, **26**
Air raids, 4
Albania, **27**
Aldermaston, **33**
Alexandria, Egypt, **23**
Algeria, 48, **49**
Allied Occupation of West Germany, 10, **11**
Americanization in Europe, 10; in Asia, 12; of Japan, 12; in Latin America, 12
Animal Farm, **46**
Antonioni, Michelangelo, **35**
Arab states, 20, 21, **21**
Arabs, and Jewish settlers in Palestine, 20; nationalism, 22; U.S.A., animosity to, 12
Argentina, 38, **38**, **39**
Argentine Grand Prix, 28
Arms race, **25**
Artificial satellites, 50
Ashes and Diamonds, **34**
Asia, and films, 34; U.S.A. animosity against, 12
Aswan Dam, 22, **23**
Atlee, Clement, 56
Atomic bomb, 3, 4, 32
Atomic submarines, **33**
"Austerity" in Britain, 14
Austin Cars, 44, **45**
Australia, 48
Austria, independent in 1955, 7

Bacon, Francis, 46, **47**
Balfour Declaration, 1948, 20
Ballet, 46
Ballroom dances, 41
"Ban the Bomb": see Campaign for Nuclear Disarmament (C.N.D.)
Bannister, Roger, British athlete, 29
B.B.C. television, **43**
Beckett, Samuel, 46
"Beetle" (Volkswagen), **45**
Belgium, 10
Bell XS-1 Rocket planes, **53**
Bell Telephone Laboratories, 50
Ben-Hur, 34
Ben-Gurion, David, 56
Bergman, Ingmar, **35**
Berlin, blockade of, 8; division of, 8; Four sectors of, 8; Russian sector, 8; West Berlin, 8. See also West Berlin
Bevan, Aneurin, 56
Beveridge, Sir William, 14
Beveridge Report, 1942, 14
Bevin, Ernest, 56
Bicycle taxis, 5
Bikini Atoll, 32, **32**
Bikini bathing suit, **31**
Bingo halls, 42
"Black market", **5**
Bombing in Korea, **25**
Bonn, capital of West German state, 8
Bowling alleys, 42
Boxing, 28
Bradman, Don, 28
Brando Marlon, **44**
Braun, Wernher von, 53

Brasilia, 38
Brazil, 38
Britain, affluence in 1950s; cars, 44, **44**, **45**; and Common Market, 10; in Cyprus, 48, **49**; and Empire after World War Two, 48; Festival of, 1951, **15**; and Germany, division of, 8; and Greek civil war, **6**; immigration to, **15**; and India, 16, **16**; and Kenya, 48, **49**; Labour Government after World War Two, 14, **14**; luxuriousness, 42; nuclear power, 32, **33**; nuclear weapons, 15
British Air Force, 8, **9**
British Commonwealth, 10, **14**, 48
British Empire, **14**
British Motor Corporation, 44
British World role, **15**
Brussels Pact, 6
Budapest, 26
Buick car, **45**

Calder Hall, **33**
Cambridge University, **17**
Camus, Albert, 46
Canada, 48; and N.A.T.O., 6
Cars, private, 5, 42, 44, **44**, **45**
Central African Federation, 48
Ceylon, 48
Chewing gum, a symbol of the American way of life, **12**
Chiang Kai-shek, 18, **19**
Children, British, improved health, of, **14**
China, civil war, 18; and Korea, 18, 24, **25**; a "People's Republic", 18; Mao Tse-tung, 18, **19**; Tibet, 18
Christians, and holy places, 21
Churchill, Winston, 56; at Fulton, Missouri, **6**; rejected by nation in 1945, 12
Cinema, 34, **34**, **35**
CinemaScope, **35**
Cinerama, 35
Citröen cars, 44
Civil disobedience, in India, **16**
Civil Rights Movement, U.S.A., 37
Civil Servants, **14**
Civilian war sufferings, **24**
Clothing, 30, **30**, **31**
Coal and Steel Community, European, 10, **10**
Coal mines, British, nationalized, 14, **14**
Coca-Cola, **12**
Cockerell, Christopher, 50
"Co-existence", 3
"Cold War", **6**, 8, 36; and Korea, 24, **25**
Collective farms in China, 18
Colonial Powers (Britain and France) and Suez, 1956, 22, **22**; European, 3
Comics, 37
Common Market (European Economic Community), 10, **10**
Commonwealth: see British Commonwealth
Commonwealth Trans-Atlantic Expedition, 29
Communism, and American opposition to, 12, 36, **37**; Chinese, 18, **19**; in Czechoslovakia, 6; French, 7; Greek, 6, **6**; in Indo-China, **49**; Italian, **5**, 6, 7; Orwell's satire against, 46; and "People's Democracies", 6; Yugoslavian, 7
Communes, in China, **19**
"Communism needs a boot", **5**
Communist parties, 6; in Italy, France and Greece, 6
Computers, 50, **50**
Concentration camps, 4, 20
Confucius, 18
Connolly, Maureen ("Little Mo"), 28
Conservative Party, British, 12, **15**
Cortisone, 50
Cotton, Henry, British golfer, 28
Cricket, 28
Cripps, Sir Stafford, in India in 1942, **16**
"Crooners", 40
Crosby, Bing, 40
Cuba, 38
Cyprus, 48, **49**
Czechoslovakia, Communists in power, 6

Da'Ching Oilfield, China, **19**
Daily Express, and British Empire, 14
Dakota: see Douglas C/47 Dakota
Dean, James, 41
Decolonization, 48
de Gaulle, Charles, 48, 56
de Havilland, Geoffrey, **53**
Democracy, in post-war Europe, 10
Dien Bien Phu, Battle of, **49**
Dior, Christian, 30
Disarmament talks, 32
"Displaced persons" after World War Two, 4
Dogfights, air battles in Korean War, **25**
Dominican Republic, 38
Douglas C/47 Dakota, and airlift to West Berlin, **8**, **9**
Dr. Zhivago, 46
"Drainpipe" trousers, **30**
Dresses, sack, 31; sheath, 31; **31**; trapeze, 31
Duffle coats, 20
Dulles, John Foster, 56
Dutch East Indies, 48, **48**

East Berlin, capital of East German state, 8
East German state, 26; founded, 6, 8, **8**; and West Berlin, **7**
Eckford, Elizabeth, **37**
Electronics, 50
Eden, Anthony, 56
Egypt, 20, 22, **22**
Eisenhower, Dwight, 36, **36**, **37**, 56
E.O.K.A. (Greek Cypriot Resistance Movement), **49**
Europe, 3, 4; "Americanized", 12; division of, 6; Eastern, 6; films, 34; luxuriousness, 42; Marshall Plan, 10, **10**, 12, **12**; supermarkets, 42, **43**; tension in 1948-9, **7**
European Cup Football, 29
European Economic Community: see Common Market
European Economic Co-operation, Organization for (O.E.E.C.), 10
Everest, Mount, 29
"Existentialists", 46, **46**
Exodus (Jewish refugee ship), 20

"Fair Deal" Laws in U.S.A., 36
"Fall-out" (radioactive dust), 32
Fangio, Juan, **28**
Fellini, Federico, 35
Ferranti Mark I computer, **50**
Fiat cars, 44
Fonteyn, Margot, **47**
Football, international champions, 29
France, and Citröen car, 44; and Common Market, 10; empire dissolved, 48, **49**; "Existentialists", 46, **46**; Fourth Republic, 10; and Germany, division of, 8; "New Wave" films, 34; railways reconstructed, **10**; television, **43**
Fury, Billy, 40

Gaitskell, Hugh, 56
Gatour Airport, West Berlin, **9**
Germany, and Common Market, 10; division of, 6, 8; under Hitler, 4; jet planes, 52; V2 rocket, 52, **53**; Volkswagen car, 44, **45**; after World War Two, 4
German Democratic Republic, *see* East German State
German Federal Republic, 8; economic miracle, **10**, 42; *see also* West Germany
Ghana, 48
Ghandi, Mahatma, **17**, 56

G.I. (American Serviceman), 12, **12**
Giacometti, Alberto, 46
Gingham frocks, **30**
Glider Tug Planes, **8**
Goddard, R. H., **52**
Goering, Hermann, suicide of, **4**
Golf, 28
Gomulka, Wladislaw, **27**, 56
"Great Leap Forward", **19**; *see also* Mao Tse-tung
Greece, civil war after World War Two, **6**
Greek Resistance Army (E.L.A.S.), **6**
Grivas, George, **49**
Grut, Willy, Swedish athlete, **28**
Guatemala, and U.S.A., 12
Guerillas, and modern armies, **49**
Gulf of Akaba, **23**

Haley, Bill, and his Comets, 40
Halliday, Johnny, 40
Harwell (atomic research centre, Britain), **33**
Harrow School, **17**
Hawthorne, Mike, racing driver, **28**
Health Service, British, 14
Herzl, Theodor, Jewish journalist and Zionist, 20
Heyerdahl, Thor, 29, **29**
Hillary, Sir Edmund, 29
Hillman cars, 44
Hindus in India, 16, **16**, **17**
Hinton (atomic research centre, Britain), **33**
Hire-purchase, 42
Hiroshima, destroyed, 4, 32
Hitler, Adolf, 4
Holly, Buddy, 40
Hollywood, 12, 34, **34**; labour troubles, **37**
Hovercraft, **50**
Humber cars, 44
Hungary, 26, **26**
Hydrogen bomb, 32, **32**

Iceland, **12**
Inchon, Korea, 25
India, and films, 34; immigration to Britain, 15; independence, 16; Nehru as Prime Minister, 17
Indo-China, 48, **49**
Indonesian Republic, 48, **48**
"Iron Curtain", 6, **6**, 8, **10**
Israel, founded in 1948, 20, 21; and Suez, 22, **23**
Italy, and Fiat cars, 44, **44**; films, 34, 35; Libya lost, 48; Moravia, Alberto, 46; stability in 1948-9, 10; Trieste, dispute with Yugoslavia over, **7**; after World War Two, **5**; and Common Market, 10

Jaeger, C. E., **53**
Jailhouse Rock, **40**
Japan, American influence on, 12, **12**; Britain, propaganda against, **16**; and China, 18; films, 34; industrial production, **42**; Korea lost, 48; and nuclear weapons, 32, **32**, **33**
Jerusalem, (holy city), 21, **21**
Jiminez, Venezuelan ruler, 38
Jinnah, M. A., **17**
Jiving, **41**

"Kansas-Wyoming" Line, Korea, **25**
Kanjii, Mau Mau Marshall, **49**
"Keep Death off the Road" posters, **45**
Kenya, 48, **49**
Kenyatta, Jomo, **49**

Kikuyu, and Mau Mau, **49**
King David Hotel, Jerusalem, 20
King, Martin Luther, 37, 56
Kon-Tiki expedition, **29**
Korea, 3, 24, **24**, **25**; independence after World War Two, 48
Koroiev, S., **53**
Khrushchev, Nikita, 26, **27**; visits U.S.A., 36, 57
Kubitschek, President of Brazil, 38
Kurosawa, Akira, 34

.aika, **53**
a Strada (The Road), **35**
.abour Party, British, 10; and nationalisation, 14, **14**; and the "Welfare State", 14
.abour-saving devices, 42
.atin America: see South America
.aunderettes, 42
.eague of Nations, and Israel, 21
.ebanon, 48
.e Corbusier, **47**
.eg irons, **14**
.ewis, Jerry Lee, 40
.iberace, **41**
.iberation in 1945, 5
.ibya, 48
.ife Magazine, **43**
.ittle Richard, 40
.ittle Rock Central High School, 37, **37**
.iving standards, change in, 3
.ondon, **52**
.ong-playing records, **51**
.ouis, Joe, U.S. heavyweight boxer, 28
"Lucky Dragon" Japanese fishing boat, **32**
.unar rockets, 52
.uxembourg, in the Common Market, 10

.G. cars, 44
.acArthur, U.S. general, 24, **24**
.acmillan, Harold, British Prime Minister, **15**, 57; "never had it so good", 42
.akarios, Archbishop, 57
.alaya, 48
.anchester Grammar School, **14**
.anchuria, **19**
.an-made fibres, 30
.ao Tse-tung, 57; and Chinese civil war, 18; the "Great Leap Forward", **19**; the Long March, 1934, **19**; and Russia, **19**
.arshall Plan, 6, 10, **10**, 12, **12**
.asculine clothing, 30
.aserati 250F racing car, 28
.asina, Giulietta, **35**
.ass production, 44
.au Mau, **49**
.edical discoveries, 50
.cCarthy, Senator Joe, 36
.McCarthyism", fanatical anti-communist movement in U.S.A., 36
.alta, 22
.iddle East, prospects for peace, **21**; see also Palestine, Israel and Arab states
.IG, Soviet fighterplanes, **25**
.ilitary transport planes, **8**
.ilk, free in British schools, 14
.issiles (rockets carrying nuclear warheads), 32
.itla Pass, and Suez crisis, 22, **22**
.oon, photographed on dark side, 52
.oravia, Alberto, 46
.orris cars, 44
.oss, Stirling, racing driver, 28
.otor cycles, **44**
.ountaineering, 29
.onro, Marilyn, **35**
.urder, in U.S.A., **37**
.usical films, 34
.uslim League, **17**
.uslims, and holy places, 21; in India, 16, **16**, **17**
.ussadeq, Prime Minister of Iran, 57

Nagasaki, destroyed, 4, 32
Nagy, Imre, Hungarian Prime Minister, **27**; 57
Nasser, Gamal Abdul, and Aswan Dam, 22, **23**; and Eastern Arms, 22; and Suez Crisis, 22, 57
National Coal Board (British), **14**
National Insurance, British, 14
Nationalisation, in Britain, 14, **14**
Nationalist Party Congress, India, **17**
Nazareth, in division of Palestine, 21
Nazis, trials of at Nuremberg, 4, **4**; victims, of, 4; see also Concentration camps
Negro music, 40
Negro voting rights, 37
Negroes, in U.S.A., 37, **37**
Nehru, Jawaharlal, **17**, 57
Netherlands, in the Common Market, 10
"New Look", 30, **31**
"Nine Day Crisis": see Suez
Nixon, Richard, 36
Non-violent resistance; see civil disobedience
North America, 3
North Korea, 24, **25**
North Atlantic Treaty Organisation, 6; and U.S.A., 12; West Germany joins, 10
Notre Dame du Haut, convent of, **47**
Nottingham, racial riots at, **15**
Notting Hill, London, racial riots at, **15**
Nuclear Disarmament, Campaign for (C.N.D.), **33**
"Nuclear Club", 32
Nuclear Power, 32, **33**, 50
Nuclear Weapons, 12
Nuremberg, trials at, 4, **4**

Obsolescence, built in, 42
Oil supplies from Middle East, 22
Oklahoma, **34**
Olympic Games, 1948, **28**
Opera, 46
Orwell, George, **16**

Packaging, 42
Pakistan, founded, 16, **17**; immigration to Britain, **15**
Palestine, map 1920-48, **21**; Arabs, **21**; division of, 21
Paris, and bicycle taxis, **5**; Communist Party, 1948-9, **7**; fashion centre, 30, **31**; V2 rocket, **52**
Pasternak, Boris, 46
Pentathlon, **28**
Peron, Eva, 38, **38**
Peron, Juan, 38, **38**, **39**
Petrol shortages during and after World War Two
Poland, 26, **26**; films, 34, **34**
Poles in Britain, 4
Poliomyelitis, 50
Pollock, Jackson, 46
Pop, 40
Port Said, 22, **22**
Presley, Elvis, 3, 40, **40**
Propaganda, Japanese, in wartime, 16
Protest (students), **33**
Pusan, Korea, 25

Queues, **5** see also rationing
Quinn, Anthony, **35**
Quit India Movement, **16**

Racial prejudice in Britain, **15**
Radioactive dust: see Fall-out
Radios, portable, 50
Rationing, after World War Two, 4, 5 14; end of, in Britain, 1956, **15**

Real Madrid (Royal Madrid), Spanish football team, 29
Rebel Without a Cause, **41**
Reconstruction in post-war Europe, 10
Record-players, **51**
Red Army in Czechoslovakia, 6
Red Army, Chinese, 18: see also Mao Tse-tung, and China
Refugees, Arab, from Israeli army, **21**; in camps, 4; from East Germany, **8**
"Religious" hatred in India, 16
Renault cars, 44
Republican Party, U.S.A., 36
Rheumatism, 50
Rhythm 'n' Blues, 40
Richard, Cliff, 40
Richards, Gordon, 28
Riley cars, 44
"Rock", 40, **41**
"Rock Around the Clock", 40
Rockets, 52, **52**, **53**
Rome, 1948-9, **7**
Roosevelt, Franklin D., funeral of, **12**
Rootes cars, 44
Rosenberg, Ethel and Julius, 36
Rothko, Mark, 46
Royal Air Force (R.A.F.): see British Air Force
Russia, 26, **26**, **27**; and China, 18, **19**; Germany, division of, 8; and Korean War, 24, **25**; nuclear power, 32, **33**; Orwell's satire against, **46**; Pasternak, 46; rockets, 52, **52**, **53**; Suez, 22, **23**; wartime alliance with West, 6

Sabres, U.S. fighting planes, **25**
Sadler's Wells Ballet (Royal Ballet), **47**
San Francisco, 3
Salk vaccine, 50
Sartre, Jean-Paul, 46, **46**
Satyajit Ray, 34
Scars of war, 4
Seaside, and motor cars, 44
"Segregation", 37
"Shake, Rattle and Roll", 40
"Shooting Star" (U.S. jet fighter), **25**
Shortages, after World War Two, 4
Sinai peninsula, 22, **22**
Sinatra, Frank, 40
Singer cars, 44
Skoglund, "Nacka", Swedish footballer, **29**
Somes, Michael, **47**
"Sound Barrier", **53**
South America, 3; animosity to U.S.A., 12, 38
South Korea, 24, **25**
Soviet "satellites", 26
Spaak, Paul-Henri, 57
Space, penetration of, 3, 50, 52, **52**
"Spivs", **5**
Sport, 28, **28**, **29**
Sputniks, 52, **53**
"Square-shouldered look", 30
Stalin, Josef, 26, **27**, 57
Stalinism, **27**
Status, symbols, **44**
Stern gang, 20
"Student" styles, 30
Suez canal, 22, 23
Suez crisis, 1956, 22, **22**, **23**, 48
Sukarno, President, 48, 57
Sunbeam Talbot, 44
"Supermac": see Macmillan, Harold
Supermarkets, 42, **43**
Supreme Court, U.S.A., 37
Sweden, films, 34, **35**
Sylvia, **47**
Syngman Rhee, South Korean President, **24**
Syria, 48

Taiwan (Formosa), 18
Tape recorders, 51
Technical assistance from America, 12; see also Marshall Plan
"Teddy Boys", 30, **30**
Teenage crime, 37

Teenage "sub-culture", 30
Tegel Airport, Berlin, **9**
Television and advertising, **43**; and cinema, 34; in Europe, 42, **43**
Tempelhof Airport, Berlin, **9**
Tennis, 28
Tenzing, Nepalese mountaineer, **29**
Terrorism, Jewish, 20, **20**
The Seventh Seal, **35**
The Wild One, **44**
Theatre, 46
There's No Business Like Show Business, **35**
Thermonuclear weapons, 32
Three-dimensional cinema, **35**
Tito, Marshall, **27**, 57
T.N.T. warheads, 52
Tokyo, nuclear tests, protest against, **33**
Traffic jams, and Bank Holidays, **44**
Transistors, 50, **51**
Transjordan, and Israel, 20
Travel, 42
Troop-carriers, **8**
Truman, President, 24, 36, 57; intervention policy, **12**; and "Truman Doctrine", 6
Tsiolkovsky, K. E., **52**
Tuamotu Islands, and Kon-Tiki, 29

Unemployment, before World War Two, 14
United Nations, 3; China unable to join, 18; and Korean War, 24, **25**; and division of Palestine, 21; and Suez, 22; and U.S.A., 12
United States, 3; "Abstract Expressionism", 46; animosity to, 12; Air Force, 8; bases in Europe Asia, 12; and cars, 44, **45**; and McCarthyism, 36; and Chiang Kai-shek, 18; and communism, 36; films, 34, **34**, **35**; Germany, division of, 8; and Greek civil war, 24, **25**; luxuriousness of, 12; and N.A.T.O., 6, 12; nuclear power, 32, **32**, **33**; and Suez, 22, **23**; United Nations, funds to, 12; and World War Two, 12
"Utility" clothing, 30

V2 rocket, **52**, **53**
Van Allen "belts", 52
Venezuela, 38
Viet Minh, **49**
Violence, in U.S.A., **37**
Volkswagen car, 44, **45**

Wajda, Andrezji, 34
"Welfare state" in Britain, 14, **14**, **15**
West Berlin, 1948-9, **7**; blockade of, 8, **8**, **9**; East German refugees, **8**; "Operation Vittles", 9
West German state, founded, 6, 8; first elections: see also German Federal Republic, in 1949, 10; and Marshall Plan, **10**; and N.A.T.O., 10
West Indian Federation, 48
West Indian immigrants to Britain, **15**
Western imperialism, 18
Winter of 1946-7
Wolseley cars, 44
World Cup Football, **29**
World War Two, 3, 4, 12, **12**, 52

Yugoslavia, 27; breaks with communist block, **7**; dispute over Trieste, 7

Zionism, and Palestine, 20
Zionist Movement, 20: see also Herzl, Theodor, and Israel

Further Reading

Available in the United States and Canada:

AGAR, HERBERT. *The Price of Power*. University of Chicago Press 1957.
BALDWIN, JAMES. *Giovanni's Room*. Dial Press 1956.
  Go Tell it on the Mountain. Knopf 1953.
  Notes of a Native Son. Beacon Press 1955.
BELLOWS, SAUL. *Adventures of Augie March*. Viking 1953.
  Victim. Viking 1956.
BERGER, CARL. *The Korea Knot*. University of Pennsylvania Press, rev ed 1964.
CAPOTE, TRUMAN. *Local Colour*. Random House 1950.
  Other Voices, Other Rooms. Modern Library 1955.
  Breakfast at Tiffany's. Random House 1958.
CARSON, RACHEL. *The Sea Around Us*. Staples Press 1955.
CHAMBERS, WHITTAKER. *Witness*. Random House 1952.
COOKE, ALISTAIR. *Generation on Trial*. Knopf 1950.
DAVIS, KENT. *Eisenhower: American Hero*. McGraw-Hill 1969.
FREIDEL, FRANK. *America in the Twentieth Century*. Knopf, 3rd ed 1971.
GINZBERG, ALAN. *Howl and Other Poems*. City Lights Bookshop 1956.
GINZBERG, ELI, and HYMAN BERMAN. *The American Worker in the Twentieth Century*. Free Press 1963.
GOLDING, WILLIAM. *Lord of the Flies*. Coward-McCann 1955.
GOLDMAN, ERIC. *The Crucial Decade*. Random House 1960.
GORMAN, JOSEPH B. *Kefauver: Political Biography*. Oxford University Press 1971
HEDLEY, JOHN. *Harry S. Truman*. Barron 1974.
HOFSTADTER, RICHARD, WILLIAM MILLER and DANIEL AARON. *The American Republic (Vol. II)*. Prentice-Hall 1959.
KEROUAC, JACK. *On the Road*. Viking 1957.
LERNER, MAX. *America as a Civilisation (Vol. II)*. Simon & Schuster 1958.
LINK, ARTHUR S. and WILLIAM CATTON. *The American Epoch*. Knopf 1963.
MAILER, NORMAN. *The Naked and the Dead*. Rinehart 1948.
  The Deer Park. Putnam 1955.
  Advertisements for Myself. Putnam 1959.
MCCARTHY, MARY. *Groves of Academe*. Harcourt 1952.
  A Charmed Life. Harcourt 1955.
MCCULLERS, CARSON. *A Member of the Wedding*. New Directions 1951.
  The Ballad of the Sad Cafe. Houghton 1951.
  The Heart is a Lonely Hunter. Cresset 1953.
MORISON, SAMUEL E., and HENRY S. COMMAGER. *The Growth of the American Republic (Vol. II)*. Oxford University Press 1962.
O'HARA, JOHN. *Rage to Live*. Random House 1949.
  Butterfield 8. Cresset, Harcourt 1951.
RORTY, JAMES. *McCarthy and the Communists*. Beacon Press 1954.
SALINGER, J. D. *Catcher in the Rye*. Simon & Schuster 1951.
TAYLOR, TELFORD. *Grand Inquest*. Simon & Schuster 1954, rev ed Da Capo 1974.
TRUMAN, HARRY S. *Memoirs (2 Vols.)*. Doubleday 1955-56.
WILLIAMS, TENNESSEE. *The Glass Menagerie*. New Directions 1949.
  A Streetcar Named Desire. New Directions 1947.
  Summer and Smoke. Dramatists 1950.

Available in Britain:

AMIS, KINGSLEY, *Lucky Jim*. Gollancz 1954.
BECKETT, SAMUEL. *Waiting for Godot (A Tragi-Comedy in Two Acts)*. Grove Press 1954.
BRAINE, JOHN. *Room at the Top*. Eyre & Spottiswood 1957.
BROPHY, BRIGID, *Hackenfeller's Ape*. Random House 1954.
  King of a Rainy Country. Seckey and Warburg 1956.
CARY, JOYCE. *Herself Surprised*. Michael Joseph 1951.
  To Be a Pilgrim. Harper, Michael Joseph 1949.
  The Horse's Mouth. Harper, Michael Joseph 1950.
COHN, N. *Pop from the Beginning*. Weidenfeld 1969.
EDWARDES, M. *The Last Years of British India*. Cassell 1963.
FULLER, ROY. *Fantasy and Fugue*. Macmillan 1956.
  Second Curtain. Macmillan 1956.
GALBRAITH, J. K. *The Affluent Society*. Hamish Hamilton 1958.
HASTINGS, P. *The Cold War 1945-1969*. Benn 1969.
HATCH, J. *A History of Postwar Africa*. Deutsch 1965.
HENDERSON, J. L. (ed.). *Since 1945: Aspects of Contemporary World History*. Methuen 1966.
HOUSTON, P. *The Contemporary Cinema*. Penguin 1963.
HOPKINS, H. *The New Look: A Social History of the Forties and Fifties in Britain* Secker 1963.
LAQUEUR, W. *The Israel-Arab Reader*. Weidenfeld 1969.
LESSING, DORIS. *A Proper Marriage*. Michael Joseph 1954.
  A Retreat to Innocence. Michael Joseph 1956.
  The Habit of Loving. Crowell 1958.
MURDOCH, IRIS. *Under the Net*. Viking, Chatto 1954.
  Flight from the Enchanter. Viking, Chatto 1956.
  The Sandcastle. Viking 1957.
NETTLE, J. P. *The Soviet Achievement*. Thames and Hudson 1969.
ORWELL, GEORGE. *Animal Farm*. Secker and Warburg 1945.
  1984. Secker and Warburg 1949.
OSBORNE, JOHN. *Look Back in Anger*. Faber 1956.
PASTERNAK, BORIS. *Dr. Zhivago* (1958). Fontana 1961.
PINTER, HAROLD. *The Birthday Party and Other Plays*. Methuen 1960.
SCHRAM, S. *Mao Tse-tung*. Penguin 1966.
SPARK, MURIEL. *The Comforters*. Lippencott, Macmillan 1957.
  Momento Mori. Lippencott, Macmillan 1959.
THOMPSON, A. *The Day Before Yesterday: an Illustrated History of Britain from Attlee to Macmillan*. Panther 1971.
WILSON, COLIN. *The Outsider* (1956). Pan 1957.

Acknowledgements

We wish to thank the following individuals and organizations for their assistance and for making available material in their collections.

Key to picture positions:
(T) top; (C) centre; (L) left; (B) bottom; (R) right and combinations; for example (TC) top centre.

Associated Press *p. 4(TL), 15(CL), 49(TR) (BR), 53(TL) (TR)*.
Barnaby's *p. 30(TL) (BR), 44(BR), 57(TR)*.
B.P.C. Library *p. 16(B), 17(BR), 19(CR), 27(B)*.
Brown Bros. *p. 37(TR)*.
Bruger W. *p. 19(TR)*.
Brurekman, Nico *p. 48(L)*.
Bundesarchiv, Koblenz *p. 13*.
Camera Press *p. 18(TL), 27(TR)*.
Capa, Robert (Magnum) *p. 20/21*.
Cartier-Bresson (Magnum) *p. 18(BL)*.
Central Press *p. 12(TL), 49(BL)*.
Coca-Cola *p. 12(BL)*.
Cooper-Bridgeman *p. 47(TR)*.
Daily Express *p. 5(BL), 14(TL)*.
D.C.L. *p. 50(TL)*.
Deutsches Museum, Munich *p. 52(TL)*.
Fonteyn, Felix *p. 47(TL)*.
Foto AS *p. 29(TR)*.
Fowler, John *p. 50(BL)*.
Fox Photos *p. 6(TL)*.
Freud, Giselle *p. 46(TL)*.
General Electric U.S.A. *p. 43(TL)*.
Gibbs Propriety Ltd *p. 43(TR)*.
Goddard, Ester C. *p. 52(BR)*.
Halas and Batchelor *p. 46(B)*.

Imperial War Museum *p. 2, 6(BL), 24(B)*.
India House *p. 17(TL)*.
Jaborinsky Institute, Israel *p. 20(TL)*.
Jewish Agency, Israel *p. 20(BL)*.
Keystone *p. 5(TL) (BR), 9(TR), 27(BR), 28(BL), 42(TL), 42/43(B), 57*.
King Features Syndicate *p. 36(TL), 37(BL), 38(TL) (BR)*.
Kobal Collection *p. 3, 34(BL), 34/35, 40(B), 41(B), 44(TL)*.
Krokodel *p. 54(BL)*.
Kukrunski S.C.R. *p. 23(BL)*.
Kunstgeveber Museum, Zurich *p. 26(TL), 39*.
Lord's Gallery *p. 42(BL), 45(TR)*.
M.C.A. *p. 40(TL)*.
Ministere des Affaires Etranger *p. 56*.
Musee Royale de l'Armee, Bruxelles *p. 19(BL)*.
National Coal Board *p. 14(BL)*.
National Film Archive *p. 34(TL), 35(CR) (BR)*.
Novosti *p. 23(TR), 53(BL) (R)*.
Photo Lucien Nerve *p. 47(R)*.
Popperfoto *p. 15(TL) (BR), 28(TL), 29(BR), 30(BL), 31(BR), 32(BL), 33(TL), 43(BR), 50(BR), 51(TL), 55(TR)*.
Radio Times Hulton Picture Library *p. 14(BR), 31(TL) (TC), 41(TL) (TR)*.
Rothenberg, Ben, Israel Pub. Co. *p. 21(BR)*.
Slinn, Burt (Magnum) *p. 23(BR)*.
Sport and General Press Agency *p. 29(CL)*.
Topham, John, Picture Library *p. 44(BL)*.
Trailmobile, Chicago *p. 36(BL)*.
United Artists *p. 35(TR)*.
United Press International *p. 23(TL)*.

U.S. Army *p. 4(B), 24(TL)*.
U.S. Embassy *p. 56*.
Verlag, Hans Reich *p. 10(B)*.
Verlag, Sudd *p. 8(L), 54(TL)*.
Volkeswagon *p. 45(TL)*.

Editors
Susan Ward
Tim Healey

Project Author
Maurice Clifton

Front cover: British nuclear explosion at Maralinga, Australia, 1956.

Back cover: A satirical view of "Americanization" — the entire world is wooed by Coco-Cola.

Note: in this book all foreign words, titles of books, films, songs, etc. are in italics, e.g. *Look Back in Anger*.